Examining the Impact of Trauma

Examining the Impact of Trauma

Continuing the Conversation of Same-Sex Attraction

BRAD GRAMMER

RESOURCE *Publications* · Eugene, Oregon

EXAMINING THE IMPACT OF TRAUMA
Continuing the Conversation of Same-Sex Attraction

Resource Publications
An Imprint of Wipf and Stock Publishers
199 W. 8th Ave., Suite 3
Eugene, OR 97401

www.wipfandstock.com

PAPERBACK ISBN: 978-1-4982-9015-9
HARDCOVER ISBN: 978-1-4982-9017-3
EBOOK ISBN: 978-1-4982-9016-6

Manufactured in the U.S.A.   06/06/16

Contents

Acknowledgments | vii
Introduction | ix

1   *First, My Own Story* | 1

2   *Traumas? What, Me?* | 8

3   *Life Shouldn't Be This Difficult!* | 17

4   *The Born-Gay Myth* | 25

5   *The Way Life Should Be* | 35

6   *The Drive for Completion* | 48

7   *The Mystery of Hate* | 60

8   *The Church: The Bad and the Ugly* | 68

9   *The Church: The Good News* | 80

10   *Redemptive Suffering* | 87

11   *How God Meets Us in Suffering* | 95

12   *Be Not Afraid—Listening to an Angry Culture* | 102

13   *Elevating the Conversation* | 109

14   *Love Starts in the Family* | 117

15   *The Journey Out* | 134

     Conclusion | 143

Further Reading on Same-Sex Attraction | 145
Bibliography | 147

Acknowledgments

THE JOURNEY IN WRITING this book has been quite an adventure. For much of the time, I believed I would never actually publish it. Initially I was writing for myself, putting into words what I have learned in more than two decades of ministry. However, after much prodding and encouragement from others, I have accomplished what, to me, felt almost impossible. Impossible because this writing took place in the midst of unemployment, betrayal, the loss of both of my parents and several friends, as well as my own cancer diagnosis.

God has been my strength, my hope, and my foundation in all the storms through which I have navigated. I have shed many tears in the past few years, and he has comforted me and given me fresh perspective and new beginnings. In addition, God has provided companions who have girded me up and remained faithful through the ups and downs.

My wife, Laura, has endured more than enough these past twenty-three years. Without her constant belief in what is true, I certainly would have given up years ago. Thank you, Laura, for loving me in the calm and in the storms. Thank you for modeling how to persevere even when a light can't be seen at the end of the tunnel.

My sons, Micah and Noah, have been constant inspirations to me. Being a dad has probably been the greatest challenge I could face. I have made many mistakes and have also done some things well. Regardless of whether I succeed or fail as a dad, my sons have extended forgiveness and filled my life with joy. They have taught me much about what men need in the early years. Thank you, boys, for giving me the privilege of being your father.

My friends have been equally inspiring and have carried me when I felt all hope was lost. They've enriched my life and taught me what Jesus is like. The men I call friends include Matt Aalsma, Brian Bokhart, Chris Bruno, Michael Cary, George Donelson, Anthony Dumas, Richard Engle,

Acknowledgments

Daniel Fuller, Kyle Hufford, Nathan LaGrange, Tim Landrum, Paul Neal, Randy Sondrol, and Wolfy. Countless other men have strengthened my beliefs and my heart. God has richly blessed me with the kind of men who are hard to find in this world.

In the desert times throughout the years, there have been authors, ministers, and leaders who have led me when the church appeared to be dying. You gave me hope that the Spirit is still alive and present. To these special people, I extend my gratitude: Dan Allender, Mario Bergner, Francis Chan, Andy Comiskey, Larry Crabb, John Eldredge, Janelle Hallman, Henri Nouwen, Leanne Payne, David Platt, Gary Thomas, and the authors of *Living from the Heart Jesus Gave You*. You are unaware of the impact you've had on my life, but I want to I express to you now that your lives have nourished and fed me well.

Special thanks to Jason and Christina Howe, Stephen and Carol Englehardt, Carmel Fey, Brian and Brenda Fike, Chris and Christine Gorz, Laurent Rupp, and countless others who have faithfully prayed and financially supported this project. A big thanks also to Chris Smith and Dorcas Cheng-Tozun for your editing gifts and preparation of the manuscript. All of you have been a significant part of bringing this book to fruition.

Last but not least, to the courageous men and women who have trusted me with your hearts, I express my deepest gratitude. In the past twenty-four years, you have bled, wept, celebrated, and taught me. Your life stories, insights, failures, and successes have all contributed to what I now understand about us as humans. This book would not have been written without each of you teaching me in our times together. Often the encouragement to write came from many of you. Thank you for allowing me to journey with you.

Introduction

THE BEAT OF THE music in the bar was mesmerizing . . . strong. Young men, middle-aged men, and older men were crowded into the room, all looking for someone or something. One young man asked me about the button I wore, which had the name of my ministry on it, along with my first name and an image of a cross.

I replied with my memorized response: "We're here to talk to anyone who wants to talk about God."

He immediately shot back at me, *"Well, do you think homosexuality is a sin?"*

I began ministry twenty years ago by walking the streets of Chicago, seeking to help those trapped in male prostitution. In the mid-1990s, the Chicago police were reporting that, for every female prostitute, there were three male prostitutes in the city. Men involved in prostituting were mostly young, lost, homeless, and broken. Walking the streets was our first contact but meeting these young men often meant going into bars frequented by men with same-sex attractions, or those identifying themselves as gay.

What I learned in these bars—places that were supposedly danger-ous—is that there are many people who are hurting there, real people with real feelings. Unfortunately, words like *male prostitute* can put a label on someone, identifying a young male by his behavior. Over time, though, I began to see that these young men weren't *prostitutes*; they were hurting young males looking for someone to truly care for them and love them. The gay men in the bars were not very different in terms of their hearts' desire: to be loved. Regardless of which bar I was in, the people were often the same, and, regardless of the place, I would invariably be asked the question: "Do you think homosexuality is a sin?"

When I was younger and less wise about how to respond, I would answer, "I believe God says that homosexuality is a sin." Next thing I knew,

I was being yelled at, or argued with, or just abandoned as the conversation ended abruptly. What I learned was that the goal wasn't to speak the truth anytime I felt like it, or where it seemed like I *must* answer the question. The goal was to be patient and to learn when to speak truth at the right moment. Sometimes that meant waiting for the next time we talked. Most of the time, I learned to listen first, to hear someone's story.

The night I changed my approach came when one man asked me if I thought homosexuality was a sin. Rather than state what I believed, I responded, "Why do you care what I think about homosexuality? I just met you. What does it matter what I think?"

This young man described how he had met people like *me* before and how they told him he was going to hell. He explained how he felt completely disrespected and devalued. As he shared, I couldn't help but agree with him. I then said, "I want to ask for forgiveness for any Christian that has mistreated you. Would you forgive me?"

I think he was stunned at first; however, his attitude completely changed. Rather than being defensive, his countenance softened and he thanked me for asking. He said no one had ever asked him that before.

Twenty years ago, the conversation was already in full swing between Christians and the gay community. Was homosexuality really a sin? Are individuals with same-sex attractions doomed to an eternity in hell? The traditional Christian view is that all those participating in homosexual behavior are definitely unsaved and going to hell. How these thoughts and discussions have divided many strangers, let alone friends and family members! The many stories from gay men, lesbians, and transvestites I've heard reveal the pain in the lives of those in the gay community and how they have been impacted by the church.

My connection with the gay community was minimal up to this point and hearing what they shared opened my eyes to much that I did not know or understand prior to this time. Even though talking with members of the gay community was a new experience for me, my personal struggle with same-sex attraction was something we certainly had in common.

Most of my initial conversations were full of listening and hearing stories. Eventually, though, I would end up sharing about my faith in Jesus Christ and how that primary relationship brought a transformation in my sexual desires such that I was not attracted to men anymore.

My story is not very common but it is real. It is *my* story.

Over my twenty years in ministry, I have read many books on the issue of homosexuality, both from a gay-affirming and traditional Christian perspective, as well as hundreds of newspaper and research articles. Much of what I read is repetitive, but each piece of information adds additional layers of insight. Many people have asked me to write a book, but early in my ministry experience I couldn't see what I could possibly contribute to the dialogue. After years of listening, reading, and counseling, I think I am finally ready to add my thoughts to the discussion.

I know much of what is going on now is a silencing of the conversation and the pressure to only speak if one accepts same-sex attractions as being okay with God and the culture. But I'm not ready to be silent yet. There are thoughts and feelings I must share before I'm no longer allowed to express what I believe.

But before I dive into these thoughts, I'd like to share a few caveats:

1. I am writing to the Christian community.

The thoughts I offer in this book are for those whose faith lies in Jesus Christ alone and those who desire to follow him with their lives. Perhaps some will pick up this book that do not have a faith at all or do not believe in Jesus Christ. These words are not for you. You are free to live as you want. Read these words knowing that there is no judgment here against you or how you choose to live. It's none of my business how you live. My prayer is that I will be gentle and humble. This doesn't mean that strong words cannot be expressed, but the manner in which I communicate is very important. Otherwise I'm only making a lot of noise (1 Cor. 13:1–4).

2. I don't know everything there is to know about everything.

Anytime you feel I am coming across as knowing everything, understand that I have weaknesses and am still learning. Hopefully, I will give enough examples of my failures in this book to support this perspective. I have twenty years of experience of working with people who have struggled sexually or are comfortable with their sexuality. This experience brings with it a certain expertise. Wisdom does not necessarily come with education. As Christians, we should remember that education can aid in adding tools to your tool belt in dealing with life, but wisdom comes from the Lord (Prov. 2:6; James 1:5). You can have a PhD and have little or no wisdom. You can also have absolutely no education and be extremely wise. Traveling around the world can help you see that some people with no education, living in extreme poverty, have much to offer the world through their own wisdom. My hope is to contribute a little to the discussion on homosexuality.

3. The use of the terms gay, lesbian, transgender, queer, bisexual, along with any other term identifying and clarifying one's sexual desire or identity, are terms with which I disagree.

I am in agreement with Jenell Paris's perspective on these terms, expressed in her book *The End of Sexual Identity*. In this excellent book, she addresses the fact that terms like *heterosexual* and *homosexual* only began being used in the late nineteenth century by medical researchers, and that they weren't used in mainstream US print until the 1930s.[1] Prior to this time, no culture used these terms in reference to sexual identity. Any terms used were translated in terms of explaining behavior rather than placing an identity on a person. Her discussion addresses the fact that applying sexual identity labels is degrading to us as human beings. It does not represent at all the essence of who we are. As she appropriately states, "God created sexuality. People created sexual identity."[2]

My preference is not to use these terms because I believe they diminish who we are as valuable human beings created by God. But for the sake of brevity and avoiding confusion, I will use these cultural terms when referring to individuals with opposite or same-sex attractions. And for the sake of simplifying the discussion, I will mostly be using the terms *gay* and *straight* rather than the myriad of terms used at present. I know this can cause people to feel not included or it can come across as limiting the discussion. I am looking to make relevant points that apply to all rather than get all of the cultural terms correct.

4. Throughout the book, I may make reference to the term sexual brokenness.

This term refers to any sexual behavior that falls outside of sex between a man and a woman in the context of marriage. I do take a traditional,

1. Paris, *The End of Sexual Identity*, 42.
2. Ibid., 75.

biblical perspective on sexuality: sex is reserved for a man and woman in the context of marriage, and celibacy should be expected for those who find themselves unmarried. I believe that *all* people are broken in one way or another and that includes our sexuality (Rom. 3:23). Sexuality has been impacted significantly ever since sin entered the world through Adam and Eve, along with all other thoughts, intentions, and behaviors of human beings.

The term *sexual brokenness* does not determine one's value, though. Often I see Americans being defensive in response to the idea that we are "broken." But the Bible is not shy about stating that we are a mess! Jeremiah states that "the human heart is the most deceitful of all things, and desperately wicked. Who really knows how bad it is?" (17:9). We are also told that no one is good, not even one (Rom. 3:9)! However, this does not determine our value. In Psalm 8, David specifically states that human beings are just a little lower than God and that we are crowned with glory and honor (v. 5). The fact that God sent Jesus Christ to die for us to save us from our sins should also clearly communicate that we matter. We are valuable! Paul states in Romans 5 that

> most people would not be willing to die for an upright person, though someone might perhaps be willing to die for a person who is especially good. But God showed his great love for us by sending Christ to die for us while we were still sinners. And since we have been made right in God's sight by the blood of Christ, he will certainly save us from God's condemnation. For since our friendship with God was restored by the death of his Son while we were still His enemies, we will certainly be saved through the life of his Son. So now we can rejoice in our wonderful new relationship with God because our Lord Jesus Christ has made us friends of God. (vv. 7–11)

Believe that truth! No matter how messed up you may feel you are, you are deeply loved by God. My sons fail regularly and often do not live up to the standards I would like them to, but they are still my sons. I love them dearly and do not equate their behavior with what they are as beautiful young men. They have wonderful personalities and gifts, and their sinful behavior never tarnishes how I see them as precious. *Know* that God sees you even better than how I view my sons!

5. One of my reasons for finally putting what I believe into words is my view of the public discussions on homosexuality.

I believe the gay community, the American culture, *and* the American church have some major gaps in fully and properly addressing the issue of gender identity. Some good things have been stated and clarified, but there are still gaps. We need a fresh perspective, another way to think, a third or fourth path to walk. There are gaps to be filled. Perhaps my words can aid in this journey of filling gaps and offering a fresh path to walk.

My perspective is consistent with that of the authors of *Living from the Heart Jesus Gave You,* a book coauthored by five Christian psychologists and therapists who have worked with people for over thirty years. They state that a person's physical age does not determine his or her emotional maturity.[3] In addition, they state the following: "As a whole, our American culture does poorly in the area of maturation, and sadly enough, the majority of our population probably operates at the infant or child level of maturity."[4]

They explain specifically what they mean by these maturity levels, and I happen to agree with them. After twenty years of counseling individuals with various struggles, I've seen how the American church has been influenced by the immature level of the American culture. We bring to our faith childlike reasoning. The author of Hebrews challenged the believers to move beyond drinking milk to eating solid food (5:11–14).

In like manner, I want to challenge the church to move beyond drinking milk to eating solid food. The issue of homosexuality has exposed how we have become stuck in drinking milk because of the immature way in which we have related to gays and lesbians, as well as to the rest of the world. Throughout the book, I will be referring to what immature behavior looks like and how we can move on to maturity. If it weren't for mature believers speaking into my life and correcting me, I wouldn't be able to offer any insights into maturity. I am grateful for these men and women who helped me to grow tremendously. I haven't arrived yet into maturity. I still have a long way to go.

3. Friesen et al., *Living From the Heart Jesus Gave You,* 19.
4. Ibid., 27.

6. And finally, when I speak about same-sex attractions, I am not talking about an abstract issue.

I am talking about myself. Writing this book has been an emotional journey for a number of reasons. For one, I am remembering my own story and the pain that came with identifying as gay. Two, I remember the stories of many of the people with whom I have spoken and counseled, and I remember the pain and struggle they have faced and how often they have not been loved by the church. Third, I am also reminded of God's amazing love for me. When I look at my life and see how he has transformed me and how he continues to do so, I am amazed at his incredible love and grace and mercy. We serve an amazing God, and I don't want anyone to escape knowing the Lord of all, Jesus Christ. He is the best thing that *ever* happened to me!

Brothers and sisters, the world is desperately seeking guidance and leading and that can only happen as we mature in the things that Christ commanded: predominantly loving God and loving people. We can grow in loving those with same-sex attractions in a way that honors Christ and values those who are also created in the image of God.

1

First, My Own Story

I GREW UP IN a Christian home. My parents were faithful Christians. They remained married until my mother died a couple of years ago, so I grew up in a family where my parents were both present. My mother and father were neither abusive nor were they addicted to alcohol or drugs. They remained faithful to one another and continually provided for my brothers and me. One element that was lacking in my family, however, was our inability to emotionally connect well with each other.

My father was emotionally very distant. Rarely did he spend time with my brothers and me. We rarely spoke to each other. When I checked with my brothers about what they remembered with regard to relationship with my father, they both stated that they pictured him sitting at the dinner table staring. Whenever he wanted something passed to him, he would point at it and grunt, meaning that we needed to pass the food to him. I can count on one hand the number of times my father spent time with me, just he and I.

One specific memory I have of my father was when I was six years old. My father was driving me to the grocery store because it was my birthday. Just he and I were in the car, and I believe I remember this memory because it was the first time I really felt a strong desire for him to speak to me. In addition, I wanted to talk to him but felt completely frozen. All the way to the store and back, not one word was exchanged between us. Understanding child development now, I know that silence always communicates a negative message to a child, whether the parent desires to do so or not. A child longs to be pursued and sought out, to be known and understood. Because my father did not practice these behaviors, I concluded he did not love me. I grew up feeling distant, unloved, and unaccepted.

Growing up in the church, I heard weekly of God's love for me. Since I felt so unloved elsewhere, I was really drawn to Jesus.

During my school years, I enjoyed learning but did not connect well socially with boys my age. Often I would be called "sissy" and left out of games they would play at recess. From third grade on, I began to feel very lonely in school. Only when I went home would I feel safe and accepted by my mother.

When I was in seventh grade, my family moved from Illinois to Nebraska because my father took a new job. This move was very traumatic for me. The teasing I previously received at school progressed to abuse. Every day was a frightening experience for me. Most days I would cry myself to sleep and be sick to my stomach in the morning. I was not outgoing and did not make friends easily. From seventh to ninth grade, I ate lunch by myself at school every day.

Alfred Adler was a well-known Australian psychotherapist and founder of the school of individual psychology. In writing about Adlerian thought, Thomas Sweeney published a book discussing this form of counseling. He explains that Adlerians believe that children are usually excellent observers, but they are often poor evaluators and interpreters of their experiences.[1]

Throughout my childhood and adolescent years, I observed well. Boys who were good in sports were the ones who got acceptance and attention. Those who were aggressive and tough were safe from being ridiculed and harmed physically, and were affirmed for being tough. My conclusion was that if I was a *real* boy, I needed to be good at sports, aggressive, muscular, emotionally cold and distant. This was an inaccurate conclusion about masculinity, but, again, children are poor interpreters. From what I observed, I truly was not a male. My body said one thing but everyone else communicated that I was *not* a boy; and I took their counsel to heart.

All of this emotional turmoil caused me to question where God was and why no one else at church seemed to wonder about God's abandoning them. No one else at church seemed to have problems because rarely did anyone share a problem. Perhaps there might be a prayer request about someone's physical illness but there were no prayer requests for struggling with depression or sexual behavior outside of God's plan.

---

1. Sweeney, *Adlerian Counseling and Psychotherapy*, 11.

By this point, the rejection I felt from my father and males at school consistently communicated to me that males were not safe and that I was not one of them. This also influenced how I felt about God. Since I saw him in a male image, I concluded that he was cold and distant as well. I became very depressed and despondent about my life. At times I was suicidal and wondered why I was here.

My sexual desires developed, as it does normally for teenagers, and I was frightened because my attractions were exclusively for men. Boys called me a "fag" in junior high and high school. I didn't even know what the term *fag* meant until I looked it up in the dictionary. Hearing what they called me frightened me because I never told anyone that my attractions were toward males and yet they seemed to know. Feeling rejected and not feeling like I fit in caused me to question my gender identity. I never progressed to the point of calling myself homosexual, but my attractions were exclusively for the same sex. Calling myself "gay" would be like putting a nail in the coffin for me because I could never see myself being happy as a gay person. The way I was treated by males proved that I could not live a happy life.

In my second year of college I came to a crossroads. I made a bargain with God that if he didn't change my life, I would kill myself. At that time, I spoke with the youth pastor of my church whom I trusted enough to be honest for the first time in my life. I met with him and shared how I felt about my life, how depressed I was, how rejected I felt, and all the guilt I felt about my sexual struggles. I was not courageous enough to say to whom my sexual attractions were directed but said my struggle was with masturbation. He shared with me that I did not have to be good enough for God, that the very reason I needed God was because I could never be good enough and that I needed Jesus to make me righteous before God. Ephesians 2:8–9 became very clear to me as this youth pastor spoke. This passage states, "For it is by grace you have been saved, through faith—and this not from yourselves, it is the gift of God—not by works, so that no one can boast" (NIV).

I went home and asked Christ into my life. I grew up Baptist and had been baptized as an eleven-year-old, but I had little understanding of what it meant to be saved.

After I asked Christ into my life, my life changed dramatically. I didn't know the first thing to do, but God had a plan. The youth pastor I shared with left the church and someone else took his place. The new youth pastor was a young believer himself and had just graduated from college. We were acquainted with each other but I had no relationship with him.

He asked me one Sunday if he could disciple me. I was attracted to him so I said yes. My intentions were not pure, but little did I know how God would take my impure intentions and use them for good. This youth pastor was the first man who loved me in a godly, healthy way. Never had a man cared for me so well. He taught me how to read the Bible and pray with complete vulnerability with God. He would hug me and tell me he loved me. None of this was unhealthy. He never struggled with same-sex attractions. In fact, he was open about his struggle with lust for women. Healthy physical affection was part of his normal world but it was completely unfamiliar to me. I loved the affection and ate it up, feeling that it was one of the ways he affirmed me on a regular basis. He was the first of several men that God led into my life.

After following Christ for thirty years and growing spiritually, I can honestly say that I am completely free from same-sex attractions. When I state this, I'm not saying I have attractions and just don't act upon them. I'm saying that I can look at men and no longer imagine them being naked or fantasize about having sex with them. My heart no longer pounds when I'm around an attractive man, wishing I could have him or be like him. I no longer feel like an outsider with men but firmly believe I *am* a man.

My relationships with the godly men God led in my life were the most significant aspect of healing in that part of my life. At the time I did not understand fully what I needed but God knew and provided men who knew how to love well and disciple me in my faith. Their love was essential in meeting my emotional needs that had been unmet for years. Looking back on my life, as well as reading others' testimonies about coming out of homosexuality, I saw that God was healing the parts of my heart that were at the foundation of why I developed same-sex attractions in the first place.

As I grew spiritually in my church, I became very involved in ministry. I served as a youth intern for a year and led a Bible study for international students the following year. After I graduated from college, I spent a summer in Japan on a mission project with Campus Crusade for Christ (now called Cru). When I returned, I worked in a home for runaway teenagers and a boys' group home. I've been an infant-toddler teacher and a preschool teacher as well. My undergraduate degree is in human development.

Once I knew that I wanted to work in full-time ministry, I decided to go to Moody Bible Institute in Chicago. I took one full year of courses and graduated with a certificate of biblical studies. My original plan was to go overseas and be a missionary, but God changed my path. I eventually became involved in full-time ministry with Breakthrough Urban Ministries in Chicago. Little did I know that God had a plan to use what was once broken in me—my sexuality—to help others who were struggling and desiring transformation in their own lives.

For six years I worked with men involved in prostitution on the streets of Chicago and went into gay bars, sharing the gospel of Jesus Christ. Starting out with Emmaus Ministries, our tactic was not to approach anyone in the bars but to simply be present and pray for opportunities to share the gospel. We also wanted to offer help to males seeking to get out of the world of prostitution, drugs, and homelessness.

After a couple years of doing street outreach, men in my church began telling me they had unwanted same-sex attractions and asking if I could help. Initially I began one-on-one discipleship with these men, but eventually so many men approached me that I started a couple of support groups for sexual strugglers. In addition, I was contacted by a chaplain who ministered in Cook County Jail. He was seeking someone to help him minister to men who professed a faith in Christ yet struggled with sexuality issues or had AIDS, and were looking for support. So I led a support group there during my time of ministry in Chicago.

While I was in ministry in Chicago, I met my wife, Laura, at the church I attended. We dated and got married in 1993. In 2015 we celebrated twenty-two years of marriage. During this time, we had two sons and I have had the privilege of watching firsthand what boys need in order to grow up and become healthy men. I was nervous about having boys, but God knew what he was doing when he blessed me with these two awesome sons. Even though I've been free from same-sex attractions, being married and being a parent has taught me a lot more about the maturation process of a believer. I have much to learn about what it means to love people, including my wife and sons. Constantly growing and learning is the norm for believers, not growing and then resting in the fact that you are complete.

My wife is originally from Indianapolis, so we would drive back and visit family in Indy. One time I sensed God leading us to minister in Indiana, and my wife stated that she had no intention of moving. So I struck a bargain with God that if this was *his* desire for us as a family, then he needed to make that clear to my wife and convince her. I didn't bring the subject up again for six months but just prayed. After six months, my wife came to me and stated that she felt compelled to move to Indiana. I knew that God was calling us there.

We moved to Indiana in 1998, and for eight years, I was executive director of Hope & New Life Ministries in Indianapolis, Indiana. Through this ministry, I led support groups for Christian men and women seeking help with sexual addiction issues, predominantly unwanted same-sex attractions. In addition, I continued doing a lot of public speaking about homosexuality that I had begun in Chicago. Part of my ministry responsibility, I believed, was educating churches and ministries on the issue of sexual brokenness.

The pastor of the church where I was an elder approached me at one point, encouraging me to consider being a pastor. After much leading and prayer, God opened the door for me to pastor a small, Sunday evening church plant out of my home church. A normal Sunday evening service encompassed anywhere from forty to seventy regular attendees. About 40–50 percent of those coming were homeless, 10–20 percent were individuals struggling with same-sex attractions, 40–50 percent non-white, 50–70 percent single, and the rest of us a mix. Never had I been in such a diverse group of people in church. I used to tell friends or anyone interested in coming to a service that they would *not* be comfortable in my church— guaranteed! Bringing such a diverse group of people together is, what I believe, what God intended with the church. However, a diverse group of people means lots of challenges as we learn how to understand and know one another. I soon began to learn that much of what I taught to those with same-sex attractions is actually quite applicable to everyone.

I think it's important for you to know that I have also lived in urban settings for over twenty years. Both in Chicago and then in Indianapolis, my wife and I have worked and lived in poverty-stricken areas. The kind of poverty we are talking about is different than the severe poverty experienced in other parts of the world, but, according to American standards, we have lived in neighborhoods people often refer to as "the ghetto." Living among predominantly African Americans, and among those who are poor, has been an important part of our learning and growing. My family has learned what it means to step outside of our prejudices and seek to know and understand others who may have very different backgrounds. At the same time, I have also learned that what is at the core of those with same-sex attractions is *also* quite applicable to those living in poverty.

Throughout my twenty years of ministry, I have learned what is at the heart of all human beings. Talking about homosexuality is not just talking about a select group of people but actually talking about what is at the heart of every person deep within. My hope is that, throughout this book, you will begin to understand not only the issue of same-sex attraction, but you will also understand more fully what it is like for all of us as human beings to grow and mature in Christ, emotionally and spiritually.

2

Traumas? What, Me?

FOR THE PAST TWENTY years, I've heard hundreds of stories regarding men's and women's struggles with same-sex attractions. I've also read and heard arguments that same-sex attractions are not caused by any one or two factors, supporting the idea that perhaps one is born with homosexual attractions. Those who affirm gay and lesbian as identities will advocate that all the arguments explaining the causes of same-sex attractions are ill-supported or unfounded. Justin Lee, in his recent book, *Torn: Rescuing the Gospel from the Gays vs. Christians Debate,* briefly addresses theories on the causes of same-sex attraction, including biological hypotheses. Although he never clearly states in the book that the cause is definitively biological, he does make statements without substantiation. For example, here are some statements that are made without support in his book:

- ". . . studies show that the majority of gay people weren't [sexually abused]."[1]

- "According to [psychologist and researcher on same-sex attraction Dr. Irving] Bieber, it's impossible for a boy to turn out gay if he has a warm, loving relationship with his father. Yet, that's exactly what many gay men had and continue to have to this day."[2]

1. Lee, *Torn,* 55.
2. Ibid., 57.

8

- "Many researchers now believe that these different brain structures help explain why some people are attracted to the same sex instead of the opposite sex—their brains may truly be different from birth."[3]

- "Many scientists now believe that sexual orientation is related to the hormone levels a baby experiences during its development in the womb."[4]

All of these statements are without support. Am I to just believe whatever Lee writes without his supporting these statements with the scientific research he seems to rely on? I appreciate Lee's desire to address the issue of same-sex attractions more honestly and refute blanket statements that are made by the Christian community and gay community. There is certainly much that has been said on both sides that is poorly supported. I have found, however, that my practical, tangible experience over the past couple of decades *does* support the idea that there are many commonalities at the core of those who struggle with same-sex attraction. My beliefs come from twenty years of ministry work hearing stories and counseling individuals, as well as leading support groups.

Lee's statement that sexual abuse is not very present in those with same-sex attractions simply is not true in my experience. Of all the people I've counseled, I've consistently found that around 80 percent of women with same-sex attraction have been sexually abused and 60 percent of the men have been sexually abused. These stories are not insignificant and neither is the issue of sexual abuse and the impact it has upon a soul. At the same time, I will be the first to clearly state that sexual abuse does not *cause* homosexuality. A causal relationship is too simplistic! There are obviously straight people who also have been sexually abused, but to disqualify sexual abuse as having little impact on sexual orientation is equally simplistic and dismissive.

What I've come to understand is that most of the Christian community needs an understanding about how people grow and develop in general. We often come up with explanations for foundational matters regarding homosexuality but don't evaluate everyone else in the same manner, particularly those who *don't* have same-sex attractions. Thus, I'd like to begin with talking about our common brokenness rather than just addressing

3. Ibid., 63.
4. Ibid., 65.

same-sex attractions. After all, my work as a pastor with many people who don't identify as gay or lesbian supports the idea that we are *all* a mess!

WHAT WE ALL NEED TO KNOW

In *Living from the Heart Jesus Gave You*, the authors did a great job evaluating our culture and identifying common problems among all of us. One chapter discusses ways in which all of us are impacted by what could be identified as traumas. Traumas are experiences that interfere with our progress toward maturity. As the authors state:

> Within each person is the natural desire to pursue maturity—to reach the upper limits of one's potential. But life is more than simply reaching one's potential. If that were all, we would be no different than robots, carrying out life as though it were a series of empty exercises. As spiritual beings, there is a deep longing within each of us to exceed what we could do on our own, to be everything that God intends. That is our destiny and we get there by passing through traumas, gaining as much as we can from each of them. Traumas that do not receive healing will steadily distract our focus and drain our energy away from reaching our destiny.[5]

This journey is one that we as humans are all on. The Bible teaches that suffering is a normal experience for all of us. To deny the reality of suffering in all of our lives is to live in fantasy rather than reality. All of us enter the world with basic human desires and we all long to grow and mature. But traumas get in the way of our progress, unless we are willing to work through them and learn. No one makes it through life without at least some emotional damage caused by traumas. My guess is that many of you reading this book will not believe that you've experienced a trauma because it didn't look like you might have imagined (i.e. physical abuse, sexual abuse, etc.).

I'd like to offer you an idea to help you think differently about this matter of trauma. Many of you reading this book have grown up in American culture. While there are great strengths and benefits of living in this culture, there are also many weaknesses. One of the greatest weaknesses is that Americans are often seen throughout the world as being less relational, less loving in our relationships. I've had many conversations with individuals from Japan, China, Thailand, South Africa, Mexico, Lebanon, India,

---

5. Friesen et al., *Living From the Heart Jesus Gave You*, 59.

Saudi Arabia, or friends who have lived in other countries for a significant period of time. What I have consistently found is that Americans have a very different view of relationships than much of the world. My older son lived in Mexico for two weeks with two different families and felt like he finally found a place where friendships were valued in the way he desired. His experience with American male teenagers was lacking, often leaving him feeling pain rather than acceptance and value.

We need to start thinking differently about American culture. Perhaps the way our culture communicates relationally contributes to a great many problems that we suffer on a regular basis. My personal belief is that those who are confused sexually are highly impacted by a culture that has no idea how to love people well.

Dr. Mark Laaser, author of *Seven Basic Desires of the Human Heart,* has worked with sex addicts for many years and overcame this type of addiction in his own life. He identifies seven basic desires endemic to all of humanity regardless of culture, socioeconomic status, gender, race, and religion. These desires are:

1. To be heard and understood

2. To be affirmed

3. To be blessed

4. To be safe

5. To be touched

6. To be chosen

7. To be included[6]

No one can escape from having these desires built into each of us. My work has found that we all have these same kinds of desires. To not have these desires met will cause damage, what the authors of *Living from the Heart Jesus Gave You* would call traumas. And once again, these traumas will inhibit our progress toward maturity. One of the main reasons most Americans function at an infant- or child-level of maturity is because they have not acknowledged their emotional damage or pain, identified it, and brought resolution to it. You and I can leave traumas unaddressed in our lives and think we can grow up and be healthy, but we are merely fooling

---

6. Laaser, *The Seven Basic Desires*, 17–42.

ourselves. There are natural orders to how we all grow and mature, and we cannot change these basic requirements no matter how hard we try.

Consider the seven desires above as you look at the Trauma Tool that the authors of *Living from the Heart Jesus Gave You* give us. They have simple categories identified as Type A and Type B traumas. Let's look at Type B traumas first (bad things that happen to us):

1. Physical abuse, including face slapping, hair pulling, shaking, punching, and tickling a child into hysteria.

2. Any spanking that becomes violent, leaving marks or bruises or emotional scars.

3. Sexual abuse including inappropriate touching, sexual kissing or hugging, intercourse, oral or anal sex, voyeurism, exhibitionism, or the sharing of the parent's sexual experiences with a child.

4. Verbal abuse or name-calling.

5. Abandonment by a parent.

6. Torture or satanic ritual abuse.

7. Witnessing someone else being abused.[7]

Most of us would agree that these behaviors and wounds would be considered traumatic. We would acknowledge that emotional damage accompanies these types of experiences.

Now let's look at the Type A traumas, which are things that should have happened but didn't. Their absence also results in trauma:

1. Not being cherished and celebrated by one's parents simply by virtue of one's existence.

2. Not having the experience of being a delight.

3. Not having a parent take the time to understand who you are—encouraging you to share who you are, what you think, and how you feel.

4. Not receiving large amounts of non-sexual physical nurturing—laps to sit on, arms to hold, and a willingness to let you go when you have had enough.

5. Not receiving age-appropriate limits and having those limits enforced in ways that do not call your value into question.

7. Friesen et al., *Living From the Heart Jesus Gave You*, 75.

6. Not being given adequate food, clothing, shelter, medical and dental care.

7. Not being taught how to do hard things—to problem solve and to develop persistence.

8. Not being given opportunities to develop personal resources and talents.[8]

I find that most Americans are completely unaware that this latter list is important for a person to grow up and be healthy, let alone that not having these needs met could be considered traumatic.

I am in full agreement with the psychologists and therapists who developed this list. We as Christians can have a tangible list to help us understand what we *all* needed growing up. There are individuals I have counseled over the years who would look at the Type B list and not necessarily see those traumas present in their lives.

When I'm working with men and women with same-sex attraction, not all of them will identify bad things like sexual abuse that have happened to them. In this sense, people like Justin Lee are correct in that some gays and lesbians haven't experienced sexual abuse. What is very interesting is that all the people I have counseled, with same-sex or opposite-sex attraction, have never identified things on the Type A list as necessary needs in their lives. Yet when they see this list for the first time, they are immediately able to identify what needs in their lives were not met. They are able to say, "I have numbers 1, 2, and 5" or "I have 3, 4, and 7 from the above list." The fact that they are immediately able to identify what they lacked shows that these desires have always been present in their hearts. They've never been taught to know what they need, and no one has given them language to express their true desires within. Perhaps these needs were rarely or never valued.

My contention is that we live in a culture that has no clue that these basic desires are present in all of us. When I look at Dr. Laaser's list, combined with the list from *Living from the Heart Jesus Gave You*, I see very important information that is unknown by the majority of the population, resulting in an entire culture that functions at an infant- or child-level of relational development. If this is true, then it is *no wonder* that there are a myriad of problems that have developed in our culture and continue to remain problems or are increasing, including depression, loneliness, anxiety,

8. Ibid., 72.

anger, isolation, gender-identity confusion, sexual promiscuity, drug abuse, alcoholism, gangs, and criminal behavior of many kinds. These problems are the result of emotional traumas, as well as immature attempts to resolve our emotional pain. The only way we can overcome any of our problems, both personally and as a culture, is to acknowledge that we have these basic needs; that it's imperative to have these needs in healthy ways to be mature adults; and to bring resolution to the traumas that have resulted by not having these needs met.

Sometimes people write about how it seems like some counselors, pastors, or people ministering to those with same-sex attractions are trying to drum up problems by saying, "Aha! This is what caused your homosexuality!" But I am not interested in identifying what *caused* same-sex attraction. I'm interested in identifying, for every person with whom I counsel (those with same-sex *or* opposite-sex attractions), the need that can finally be met in healthy ways. I know that *every* person has Type A traumas of one kind or another, to varying degrees. Not everyone has Type B traumas, although these are very important to address. *Everyone* has unmet needs in our lives, especially as I look at a culture that has little understanding of how people grow and develop, and little understanding of how to truly love one another.

In further response to the idea of drumming up problems, it's important to understand another way that we human beings function. As children, we don't come into the world *knowing* what we need. We come into the world being completely immature and lacking in knowing ourselves. We need parents to help teach us what we really feel and how these feelings are linked to legitimate needs. We have to be taught about ourselves!

When addressing Type A traumas, the authors of *Living from the Heart Jesus Gave You* specifically state that this "is the way Type A traumas act—the painful feelings begin to emerge when the person sees the good thing that has been absent."[9] You and I don't always know what we need until someone puts language to an experience, or experiences, and we connect with it in our hearts. Then we can say, "Yes, that's me! That's why I feel this way! This is the reason why I behave this way!" Those of us in counseling ministries are not trying to *drum up* problems. We are finally uncovering what has always been there but remain unidentified by the client. This is no fault of his or her own; it's the result of an immature culture

9. Ibid., 70.

where parents grow up not knowing their own needs and are not able to teach their children about basic needs, growth, and development.

Here's further explanation:

> Most people find it hard to see that Type A traumas are the cause of their pain, depression, or isolation. These traumas are usually easier to remember than Type B traumas, but are less likely to be given significance. Their importance is denied, leaving persons puzzled about why they feel so awful about themselves, why they are so afraid to trust, or why they feel the continual need to prove their worth. With the significance of the traumas denied, people are at a loss to understand where the disturbing feelings come from. They often can make no sense out of the feelings, and simply place blame on themselves ("I am defective") or on their creator ("God made me defective").[10]

There are results from having traumas and also results from not identifying and healing traumas. Here are some of the common results of unresolved wounds:

1. Lack of trust

2. Suppression of feelings

3. Avoidance of pain/conflict

4. Protective mechanisms: manipulation, anger, control of environment/ legalism, addictive behaviors

5. Over-spiritualizing life

How many of you can identify with the Type A or Type B traumas? How many of you can identify with the results of unresolved traumas? If you are like the majority of us, you will be able to connect very well. I have never counseled someone without that person being able to identify emotional needs, bad things that have happened to them, as well as the results. When only looking at Type B traumas, many people cannot identify with these, but I have never seen anyone not be able to identify traumas on the Type A list, including myself. I actually had no traumas from the Type B list but I could identify five of the Type A list. These are the traumas I needed to focus on to bring healing and resolution to my life. Even after thirty years, there are still a couple of unresolved traumas I'm working on.

---

10. Ibid., 70–71.

However, this is what the Christian journey really looks like. In the next chapter, I will identify a couple of false beliefs that can inhibit our progress in resolving the impact of traumas.

3

Life Shouldn't Be This Difficult!

ONE THING I HAVE discovered in helping people is that we all develop false ways of thinking. These false beliefs are partly what contribute to our pain and confusion, and inhibit our ability to grow and bring resolution to traumas. I just dispelled one of these false beliefs in the previous chapter. At one point in my life, my belief was that life shouldn't be this difficult. I used to think that life should mostly be manageable with some occasional bumps. I remember watching a reality-TV show years ago that featured a group of people opening and working in a new restaurant. Some of the scenes were conversations that took place between the coworkers. One waiter was having difficulty handling the stress of the job and he communicated to his friend, "If I have to suffer for *one* minute, then it's not worth it! I don't need to be here!" This young man's parents did not teach him the truth!

I have come to understand this truth: life is mostly difficult and occasionally I have some nice moments. When I share this belief, some people get very discouraged because they too have fallen into this false belief. They too believe, like the waiter I just mentioned, that life shouldn't ever be that difficult. That would be true in a world where there is no sin. The reality is, though, that a world full of sin is going to be a world full of problems! Jesus didn't die on the cross because you and I had a *little problem* to address. He died because, apart from Jesus, we were desperately wicked and deceitful above all things (Jer. 17:9)!

Another reality is that most of the world actually suffers quite severely every day. Half of the world's population lives on ten dollars a day or less.

That's over three billion people! Fighting for basic survival and hoping they get to eat and have clean water is part of their daily experience. Approximately five thousand people die every day in sub-Saharan Africa from HIV/AIDS. In the United States, treating AIDS has progressed in such a manner that the disease is not an automatic death sentence like it used to be. Many people with AIDS can live for many more years after diagnosis. But five thousand people don't have access to daily basic needs and health care, even though part of the world could be the answer for that problem (i.e., you and me)!

I don't share these things to dismiss your struggles or belittle them. I share them to help us identify the false belief that life shouldn't be that difficult. This is partly the result of an affluent culture, which breeds self-absorption and closed eyes to the serious issues of the world. This is also the result of not working through internal emotional pain, of which we may not be aware, and being unable to handle any more pain because we haven't brought resolution to hurts deep down. Changing our perspective to a life of reality, which is full of problems, results in growth and maturity where we find that we're able to handle whatever comes our way—not just because we grow and mature, but more significantly because we follow Jesus Christ who gives us everything we need to face what is before us (Phil. 4:13; 2 Pet. 1:1–11). Growth and maturity, however, cannot take place without identification and resolution of traumas.

I believe that both Christians and the gay community have often belittled people with same-sex attraction. Christians simplify people's lives by saying you just need to pray and read your Bible more or that the same-sex attraction is a choice. "Make the right decision!" they say.

On the other hand, some gay activists say that those who identify as gay or lesbian are born this way. Both are belittling arguments that devalue a person and what he or she has experienced in life. We are much more complex than having one little issue that needs to be overcome or accepted. There is much more going on in each one of us that requires a lot more work to know and understand and truly love someone well. So often we are looking to formulas to "make people work" or to "fix" them. People are not machines! We are not meant to be fixed! We are meant to be loved! And to *truly* love someone, this requires much more than either you or I are willing to do naturally. Love requires sacrifice, commitment, and a death to our own selfishness and pride.

The authors of *Living from the Heart Jesus Gave You* explain that finding healing for Type A and Type B traumas encompass two different paths. They also appropriately identify that counseling *alone* helps no one! "It does no good to be honest about one's suffering in a therapist's office if that is the only arena where it is permitted. Therapy will fail if the client is restricted to being real and honest only in the therapist's office."[1] This has been my experience working with people as well.

They also observe, "Therapy can help identify Type A traumas, but it takes loving relationships for recovery. Therapy helps with the traumatizing effects of the absence of things that were needed, and loving relationships provide the essence of those things so that healing can take place."[2] Basically, the authors are stating what God has been talking about for thousands of years! God constantly calls us to *love one another.* This isn't a mild request! God made this very clear from early on that relationship is *the most important* focus of our lives! Jesus reiterated what God said thousands of years before: "You must love the Lord your God with all your heart, all your soul, and all your mind. This is the first and greatest commandment. A second is equally important: 'Love your neighbor as yourself.' The entire law and all the demands of the prophets are based on these two commandments" (Matt. 22:37–40).

WHAT'S LOVE GOT TO DO WITH IT?

After thirty years of following Christ faithfully, I have found that most Christians think they are loving people well. My contention, however, is that because we are an immature culture, we in the church know very little about loving people well. Isn't our immaturity part of the explanation why many aspects of our lives as believers are not very different from those who don't follow Christ? Why are divorce rates just as horrible as those who don't identify as Christians? Why are homosexuals not loved in the church? I have met many men and women who once used to be in the church. They didn't leave because they are just sinful and rebellious people. They left because the help they sought was not offered, and now I understand why. Most Christians don't know how to love, so we end up leaving gays and lesbians outside the church doors because they are some of the many people we have not loved well.

1. Ibid., 9.
2. Ibid., 72–73.

I've been married for twenty-two years and have been a father for over nineteen years. I've been a friend for many more years than this and served as a pastor for six years. One thing I have consistently found: I really *suck* at loving people! Through all these years, I have been slowly learning how to work through my wounds that hinder me from loving. In addition, I've been slowly identifying my sin issues that contribute to my failing at relationships. I've learned that loving people is *way* more difficult than I ever realized. This is because I was never taught well by my parents or the culture or the church. Only as I have encountered a few mature believers who taught me have I learned about love. Only as I have opened myself up to being in relationship with people with whom I have *nothing* in common have I learned about love. Only as I have humbled myself before God and let him love me through discipline have I learned about love. All of these things have taught me about love and I'm still learning. Whoever thinks they have learned how to love well is not very mature at all. They have much more to learn!

So when you hear someone say, "I tried to change my sexual attractions, but it didn't work," they are probably right. The reason isn't necessarily always because it *doesn't* work. The reason is that there is more that needs to take place than just the individual working on his or her issues. What is also required is a Christian community that knows how to love that person well because some needs are *only* met in the context of true relationship, where a person is seen, known, accepted, and loved well. Relationship is an important part of healing wounds. This doesn't necessarily explain every situation but it explains way more than I care to admit. From all my experiences in ministry, I have learned the church is in desperate need of growth and maturity in following the two greatest commandments. When we are able to live in true spiritual maturity, *then* we will be able to see transformation take place in the lives of many people, including those seeking to overcome same-sex attractions.

TIME DOESN'T HEAL ALL WOUNDS

Before I finish this chapter, I want to address one other matter. It's important that we are aware of how difficult it can be to experience healing from unresolved traumas. To the degree a person experiences any or all of the traumas, this impacts the degree of damage and what needs to be done to recover and heal. The amount of time to experience healing and growth can be quite lengthy. We need to be respectful of people by not using formulas to help them "get over" things quickly. We must follow the lead of the Holy Spirit and know a person's story.

We don't find it difficult to understand traumas that happen to us physically. Someone may be in a severe car accident and will end up in the hospital for a few months. Even though she survives, she may leave the hospital in a wheelchair or walk with a limp for the rest of her life. Why do we find this understanding difficult to apply to our emotional wounding? What's true for the body is also true for the soul. Some of us may be so emotionally damaged that we walk around with an emotional limp for the rest of our lives.

Let me give you an example. One night I was doing bar outreach with my Emmaus Ministries street partner in Chicago. My street partner was talking to another person she knew on the other side of the bar. I was watching a couple of men playing pool. One man was dressed as a woman and walked up to me, inquiring about the button with the name of the ministry that I wore. Once I stated that we were there to talk to anyone who wanted to know about God, he responded, "Get out of here! This is the way we are! You're not going to change us!" I promptly expressed that I had no intention of changing him and that I was sincerely interested in talking about God. For some reason he changed his mind, and we ended up talking for about an hour and a half.

During the course of that time, I *only* asked questions and listened. I believe you need to seek to understand first before you share anything. My goal as a believer is not to get my message out. My goal as a Christian is to know a person and to speak to the deeper issues of the heart, things that our Father in heaven cares about. When God sees that man, he doesn't see a man dressed as a woman. He sees a man in need of a Savior, just like I needed a Savior!

At one point this man expressed that he had been sexually abused for ten years by both his father and his uncle. I learned a couple of things from this moment early on in ministry:

1. The reason you don't speak first is because everyone has a unique story, and what is important to say to one person may be completely irrelevant for someone else. Again, we are not machines to be fixed. We are people to love and relate to.

2. When a moment comes where it's obvious that something needs to be said, do so very gently and humbly. You are dealing with people's lives. Wounds are present and hurt emotions accompany these wounds. So *if* you say anything, do so very gently out of respect for their story.

After I heard of this sexual abuse, I knew the Holy Spirit was giving me an open door to speak. So I walked through this door and shared gently, "There is no way that this could have happened to you and not affect your sexual identity." Part of the reason I said this is because most people, Christian or not, still believe that having sex with your dad and uncle is wrong. Secondly, he was giving me an important piece of information that was applicable to *his* story. Not the story of everyone who is gay, just *his* story. So I spoke to *his* story.

What shocked me was his response: "You know, you're right. In fact, I don't think I'm always going to be this way. I have a girlfriend and she doesn't know I do this."

I responded, "Whoa, whoa, whoa! An hour and a half ago you were telling me this is the way you are and you're not going to change. Now you're telling me just the opposite! What happened?"

He explained that when he first met me he assumed I was going to judge him and tell him he's going to hell. After I listened to him and asked questions, he realized that I cared about him. I had *earned* his trust by listening to him.

Listening is *so* important in this life. Most people don't listen. We need to learn how to develop trust in our relationships by listening a lot more and talking a lot less. Listening creates trust and safety. When this man felt safe, he told me how he really felt. Once again, this doesn't explain the cause of same-sex attractions for every gay or lesbian person. This was *his* story and what he shared was very important.

This man received physical affection from a man, mostly in the context of doing something sexual. He was meant to grow up with a father who could show lots of healthy physical affection that did not involve anything sexual. However, he began to experience physical touch at a very early age in the context of sexuality and this caused his brain to be hardwired in such a way that physical touch from a man was always or mostly sexual.

Do you understand how this can mess a child up? Do you also understand how this could have such a damaging impact on his life that he may never recover from it? I'm not saying he won't, but it's possible that the damage is so bad he may never be able to experience healthy physical affection with a man disconnected from sex. So he may struggle with these same-sex attractions until he dies. This doesn't mean that God cannot change him. Sometimes God doesn't change everything in life just because it's bad. I personally believe God wants us to know that we can't treat people any way we want to and expect not to have consequences.

I did not have the privilege of counseling this man. This conversation was the only time I saw him, so my perspective about his future is merely conjecture. Perhaps he overcame his sexual desires and functioned as a man with opposite-sex attractions.

We shouldn't be surprised if someone seeks to overcome same-sex attraction and doesn't experience the result they desire (i.e. opposite-sex attraction). Our stories and experiences will determine how much healing takes place and how long it takes. This can be a sad and discouraging part of our story. But it doesn't have to be so if we *all,* straight and gay, are walking this same path. Many people with opposite-sex attractions constantly struggle with lusting after the opposite gender. In all their efforts to work on their traumas and wounds, they experience progress but perhaps not complete freedom. They may have to keep a check on their behavior until they die. This is no different for the person with same-sex attractions.

We may not experience what we long for during our lives on earth. But, for the believer, earthly life is only a small part of our story. We have an eternity of living with our heavenly Father forever! We may not experience the freedom we seek on earth but one day we *will* be free from whatever ails us! If we cannot experience any kind of joy from this hope, then we need to go back to the basics and remember what Jesus Christ did for us. He certainly didn't *want* to experience severe suffering and die! But he was willing to do so out of his great love for us! He died so that we might live, free from condemnation from all of our sins. I think we can encourage one another to see not only what Jesus did for us out of his great love but also to make this same kind of sacrificial commitment to God. We have the same choice to walk on the path of sacrifice of our desires for the sake of following Christ. This brings a certain amount of pain, but this is temporary and fleeting compared to our amazing future! Paul reminds us of this in Romans 8 when he states clearly:

> Yet what we suffer now is nothing compared to the glory he will reveal to us later. For all creation is waiting eagerly for the future day when God will reveal who his children really are. Against its will, all creation was subjected to God's curse. But with eager hope,

the creation looks forward to the day when it will join God's children in glorious freedom from death and decay. For we know that all creation has been groaning as in the pains of childbirth right up to the present time. And we believers also groan, even though we have the Holy Spirit within us as a foretaste of future glory, for we long for our bodies to be released from sin and suffering. We, too, wait with eager hope for the day when God will give us our full rights as his adopted children, including the new bodies he has promised. We were given this hope when we were saved. (If we already have something, we don't need to hope for it. But if we look forward to something we don't yet have, we must wait patiently and confidently.) (vv.18–25)

Let's wait patiently and confidently for our freedom from sin and suffering, and to receive our full rights and new bodies. The day *is* coming, brothers and sisters! You don't have to fret! Let's encourage one another and wait together while we walk this journey!

4

The Born-Gay Myth

IN THE EARLY 1990S, the media reported on new scientific studies through-out the country that proclaimed evidence that homosexuality is genetic.[1] No longer did homosexuals have to live with the shame that they had cho-sen to make "sinful" sexual choices in their lives. They couldn't help having same-sex attractions. The new information supported the idea that the only way to address this issue was to accept and affirm homosexuality, since it was an unchangeable condition.

When I was living in Chicago in 1993, I remember seeing the headline "Gay Gene Found" on the front page of *The Chicago Tribune.* Wow! This really sparked my interest, as I had begun ministry reaching out to those in the gay community, telling them about the love that Christ has for them. The article referred to a recent study released by Dr. Dean Hamer on his research of the Xq28 chromosome.[2] Seventy-six of the homosexual males studied had a statistically higher incidence of homosexuality in their male relatives (brothers, uncles, male cousins) on the mother's side of the family, suggesting a possible link through the X chromosome. Then, in a sample

---

1. LeVay, "A Difference in the Hypothalamic Structure Between Heterosexual and Homosexual Men," 141–48; Bailey and Pillard, "A Genetic Study of Male Sexual Orienta-tion," 1081–96; Hamer, et al., "A linkage between DNA markers on the X chromosome and male sexual orientation," 321–27. For further study of the scientific research on a possible biological etiology for homosexuality, read "The Use of Scientific Research in the Church's Moral Debate," by Stanton L. Jones and Mark A. Yarhouse.

2. Hamer et al., "A linkage between DNA markers on the X chromosome and male sexual orientation," 321–27.

of forty pairs of homosexual brothers, thirty-three were found to share evidence of a variation in the same small section of the X chromosome.

The reporter did the best he could to report on these new scientific findings. However, articles questioning Hamer's research soon began appearing in newspapers around the country. *The Salt Lake Tribune* quoted Hamer as saying he didn't find a gay gene: "We knew that genes were only part of the answer. We assumed the environment also played a role in sexual orientation, as it does in most, if not all behaviors . . . Homosexuality is not purely genetic. . . . environmental factors play a role. There is not a single master gene that makes people gay . . . I don't think we will ever be able to predict who will be gay."[3] These remarks from Hamer were very different from what was originally reported. In fact, the Office of Research Integrity investigated Hamer's research based on allegations that he selectively reported his data.[4]

POPULAR THOUGHT OVER FACT

I have come to understand in recent years that Americans often believe what is popular to think rather than what is actual fact. Perhaps we are more inclined to popularity because issues are more complex than we think and require time, energy, and effort to truly understand. Martin Luther King Jr. stated once, "Rarely do we find men who willingly engage in hard, solid thinking. There is an almost universal quest for easy answers and half-baked solutions. Nothing pains some people more than having to think."[5] Perhaps we are just too lazy to put in the effort to *know* rather than *believe* before we actually *truly* know. More than likely, though, we are more tempted to believe in a path that's easier when we have already experienced pain and trauma related to the issue. Those of us who have had or still have same-sex attractions did not have an easy path getting to the place of admitting that we were gay.

The media in our culture sometimes fosters simplistic thinking by its report methods on issues like same-sex attraction. In my undergraduate years, one of my professors of family dynamics specifically stated that you could prove anything by one scientific study. Over my years of watching the morning news, I find it is a common experience to watch a report on

3. Byrd, et al. "Homosexuality."
4. Crewdson, "Study on 'Gay Gene' Challenged."
5. King, *Strength to Love*, 5.

one study stating one "fact," only to have another study revealed soon after reporting the opposite conclusion.

Scientists know that one study does not prove anything. In order for a hypothesis to become fact, numerous studies on the same research need to be conducted and the same results must be found before concluding that something is *fact*. The general population today knows there is a direct correlation between lung cancer and smoking because there have been numerous and consistent studies over many years of actual people with lung cancer that demonstrate this hypothesis to be fact. At one time, there was little to no support for this perspective. In fact, if you look at old ads for smoking, you will even see statements like "More Doctors Smoke Camels than any other cigarette!"[6] We can believe something for a very long time before finding out that this belief is not supported by evidence.

In addition, reporters often review the research or conduct interviews without themselves understanding the scientific studies. Reporters may also be influenced by the biases they bring to an interview or research. I think those who conduct the research are the best candidates for communicating what their research actually states, not reporters who interpret what they *think* the scientist or the research concludes, with only partial accuracy. I don't mean to rebuke all reporters, but I believe that poor reporting needs to be addressed, and the media needs to be held accountable for communicating false evidence, like leading an entire culture to believe that one is "born gay."

To date, there is no consistent scientific evidence that proves that homosexuality is genetic. There are individual studies that have been conducted but no consistent conclusions have emerged. In fact, Dr. Hamer's study on the Xq28 chromosome was replicated in Ontario, Canada, resulting in the opposite conclusion of the original study.[7] The website for the American Psychological Association reports that, as of December 2015, the research does not support a biological connection. In other words, they cannot say that one is "born gay." Here is the exact wording addressing the etiology of homosexuality:

> There is no consensus among scientists about the exact reasons
> that an individual develops a heterosexual, bisexual, gay, or lesbian

6. Stanford School of Medicine, "Stanford Research into the Impact of Tobacco Advertising."

7. Hu et al., "Linkage between sexual orientation and chromosome Xq28 in males but not in females," 248–56.

orientation. Although much research has examined the possible genetic, hormonal, developmental, social, and cultural influences on sexual orientation, no findings have emerged that permit scientists to conclude that sexual orientation is determined by any particular factor or factors. Many think that nature and nurture both play complex roles; most people experience little or no sense of choice about their sexual orientation.[8]

There can be no definitive statement communicating that homosexuality is a result of one's genetics. If someone wants to *believe* that a person is born gay, that is that person's prerogative, but we cannot look to research or evidence of any kind that supports this belief.

WHAT IF IT'S TRUE?

This is a question we need to ask ourselves as Christians: What *if* the scientific evidence eventually comes to the consistent conclusion that homosexuality is genetic and that someone with same-sex attractions is born that way? If there is a genetic correlation, does that mean Christians need to affirm being gay as acceptable in God's eyes?

I believe that, for the believer, it makes no difference. Even if the research supports the idea that people are "born gay," we should not be surprised. The impact that sin has had on the world impacts every aspect of life as we know it. In the words of Kay Arthur, "First, if man had not sinned, there would be no sickness. So in that sense all sickness is due to sin."[9]

I don't mean to communicate that homosexuality is a sickness. My point is that sin has impacted everything, including our biology. We wouldn't have illness and death, were it not for sin. Romans 3:23 states that the "wages of sin is death." Biology is impacted significantly so that there are birth defects, problems with chromosomes, and genetic mutations that have negative results.

My wife was diagnosed with a deadly form of leukemia, or blood cancer, in 2007. At the time she became ill, we naturally wanted to know how or why she got this disease. A team of four oncologists, who had studied leukemia for around twenty-five years, could not give us an explanation. Even today, doctors still did not know why people get leukemia. However, we do know that there is a problem that develops with cells.

8. American Psychological Association, "Sexual Orientation and Homosexuality."

9. Arthur, *Lord, I Want to Know You*, 87.

Even though we don't always know specifics, we know generally that any kind of physical defect is the direct result of how sin in general has impacted all of life, including our biology.

Also, there are Scriptures that communicate the truth that sometimes what is natural to us as humans is the direct opposite of what God desires. This is one of the major conundrums that all believers battle on a daily basis. We often desire what God does not want for us, and we don't desire what is good for us. Paul explains this problem very well in Romans 7, where he states:

> I don't really understand myself, for I want to do what is right, but I don't do it. Instead, I do what I hate. But if I know that what I am doing is wrong, this shows that I agree that the law is good. So I am not the one doing wrong; it is sin living in me that does it. And I know that nothing good lives in me, that is, in my sinful nature. I want to do what is right, but I can't. I want to do what is good, but I don't. I don't want to do what is wrong, but I do it anyway. (vv. 15–19)

DESIRING GOD'S DESIRES

One of the main reasons we need Jesus in our lives is so that he can give us new desires, the desires that God longs for us. Psalm 37:4 states, "Delight yourself in the Lord and he will give you the desires of your heart." Perhaps we as believers read this verse and think the psalmist is communicating that if you follow God, he'll give you what you want. My understanding of this verse is that if we follow God faithfully and diligently, he will place desires within our hearts that are consistent with his will.

Second Corinthians 5:17 says that we are a "new creation." Jesus died on the cross to save us from our sins, and this is a wonderful and beautiful gift. However, Jesus wants more for us than just to release us from judgment for our sins. He actually longs for followers who are willing to give up what they naturally want in exchange for what he desires, not because they are obligated but because they love him.

None of us would have trouble understanding the desire to do anything for the one that you love, perhaps a boyfriend, girlfriend, spouse, or someone else you love greatly. We are willing to make all kinds of sacrifices to express how much this person means to us: giving gifts, showing physical affection, speaking words of praise and affirmation, serving through acts of service, or spending lots of time with that person. A friend told me recently how he would do anything for his wife when they were first dating. She might ask where he wanted to go out and eat and he would say something like "Anywhere you want. I'm just allergic to shellfish." She would ask, "Do you want to go to Red Lobster?" And he would still say, "Sure." He did this because he wanted to show her how much he was willing to do for her.

When we talk about our love for Jesus, what causes us to hold back and not want to give up everything, including giving up our desires and plans for him? He suffered and died for us, even when we didn't want him, when we were set against him. He died for both those who loved him and those who hated him. This is the kind of love he longs for us to share with him and others—a love that communicates what I want doesn't matter nearly as much as what you want.

If there's anything more crazy and unfathomable than Jesus' love, I don't know what it would be. Why would a God who created everything care about someone who doesn't even want him in his life? Why would he die, knowing completely that many people would say no to him and yes to their own plans, goals, and desires? But he did do this. He did suffer and die—for me, a selfish, arrogant, self-absorbed human. I am still amazed by the death and resurrection of Jesus, which compel me to keep moving toward him rather than away. In all of my frustrations with him, I experience more and more of his lavish love and understand more and more who he is and why he does what he does. My relationship with him, however, is not quick and easy. My relationship with him grows over time, and I must be willing to give up what I want to experience more of who he is and what he does.

When it comes to the issue of same-sex attraction, if we are to keep moving in the direction of following God and his plan for sexuality, we must accept the truth that what he desires for us is greater than what our sexual desires are. We must believe that sex is not the ultimate experience we can have on earth and there is a love that goes far beyond sex and our natural desires. There are people in the Bible who experienced this very thing and share it with us so that we know there is something greater. The apostle Paul even stated that it is *better* to not be married, to not be in a relationship where sex is expressed (1 Cor. 7:1–8). He also states that whatever we suffer now doesn't even compare to the amazing experience we will have with God in the future (Rom. 8:18–25).

Are we willing to pick up our faith and follow Jesus in this way? Someone like Paul who sings songs while he is beaten and put in prison has a power of which I cannot relate. But I want to experience this life-transforming power in some small way. I want to know what it's like to not let my circumstances and desires control me so that I have to be a helpless victim of them.

IF SAME-SEX ATTRACTION IS NOT BECAUSE OF GENES, WHAT IS THE REASON?

Earlier in the chapter, I quoted the American Psychological Association's position on homosexual attractions. They specifically state, "Although much research has examined the possible genetic, hormonal, developmental, social, and cultural influences on sexual orientation, no findings have emerged that permit scientists to conclude that sexual orientation is determined by any particular factor or factors." This organization is correct in communicating that there isn't a particular *factor,* but I believe they are incorrect when they conclude that there are no particular *factors.*

Homosexuality is very complex, and how these desires develop varies among all those with same-sex attractions. However, for a little over one hundred years, psychologists, counselors, and those ministering to men and women with same-sex attractions have come to understand some common factors that make sense in the development of homosexuality.

In this book, we've talked about basic human development and what we all need. We've addressed how traumas impact us and the results of unresolved trauma. Now let's get more specific about the particular ways our history, influences, and traumas lay the foundation for same-sex attractions. Several influencing factors include:

- Poor relationship or absent relationship with the same-sex parent
- Poor relationship or absent relationship with the opposite-sex parent
- The impact of sexual abuse and other forms of abuse
- Poor relationships or lack of relationships with same-sex peers
- Confusion in understanding masculinity and femininity
- Early exposure to sexual activity
- An individual's reactions and responses to traumas/wounds

- Demonic influences, including those transferred down through family lines (I know this is a controversial issue, but I wanted to mention it, as this is a factor in some—but not all—individuals' lives.)

Through my twenty years of experience, I have yet to meet or counsel someone who has not been influenced by some combination of these particular factors. As people work on the factors mentioned above and find resolution and healing, there is an accompanying change of sexual desires.

No one can predict the extent to which one's sexual attractions will change, but this is not because sexual desires are an unchangeable condition. How much people change is largely influenced by the amount and extent of emotional wounding that has taken place in their lives, combined with their willingness to face every aspect of their journey and work through the emotional pain. No one faults people for not wanting to walk through very painful parts of their stories. But we must fully understand that if we avoid facing the emotional damage in our lives, there are natural consequences, one of them being that we will not experience the transformation that we desire in particular areas of our lives.

I mentioned in a previous chapter that I've heard and read testimonies of quite a few individuals who said they tried to change in their sexual attraction (going from homosexual to heterosexual attraction) and it didn't work. I would definitely agree with them. Doing "the work" doesn't always result in a change in one's desires. At the same time, I also know individuals who have tried but drew lines in the sand that they didn't want to cross. By drawing these lines, they limit what can happen in their own stories.

Some have said they tried to change but what that entailed was praying quietly to themselves in their rooms and not getting the answer from God that they desired. No one is to be condemned for praying. I obviously endorse praying daily to God for our needs. We must be taught, though, that there is additional work to be done along with praying. Remember, close relationships are essential to bring healing to Type A traumas. God partly answers our prayers and meets our needs through human relationships.

Some have gone to counseling or support groups while praying and doing some heart work in their lives, and have still not shifted in their sexual desires. The expectation has been that if there are underlying issues, then working on these issues *will* result in a complete change. I've even had men come to a support group actually believing that at the end of the twenty weeks they will be completely free from same-sex attractions and will function fully with heterosexual desires. I've actually had to begin these support groups with the clear understanding that this is not a twenty-five-weeks-and-you're-straight program. In fact, I don't assure them of any kind of change in their sexual desires. What I assure them is that they will meet God and face the matters of the heart that are most important.

We are not to disrespect ourselves so much by treating each other like machines to be manipulated or fixed. We are human beings created in the image of God, having great value, and should be treated as such. One way to acknowledge our value is to realize that our call is to *relate* to one another, not *fix* one another. I've come to understand that the goal is not to experience a change in one's desires. The goal is to address the issues of the heart that God cares about in our lives. His perspective is often quite different from ours. He cares about the heart while we often care about the outward appearance (1 Sam. 16:7; Ps. 139:23–24). Our struggles and issues *reveal* that there are matters of the heart to address and the path to navigating through our hearts is not formulaic and simplistic. We are valued human beings with a Creator who relates to us uniquely and specifically. His desire is for our hearts. *We* are the ones who want results and life to work the way *we* want.

In one of my support groups, Andrew (not his real name) shared how he grew up with nine stepfathers, all of whom were alcoholic and abusive. All of these stepfathers were in his life before his fifteenth year of life! He shared horror stories of watching them abuse his mother. In one instance, he took a gun and threatened to shoot his stepfather if he didn't stop beating his mother. At the age of fifteen, Andrew got sick of living in a violent home where no love was experienced. He began his life on his own at fifteen with no high school diploma, no job, and no place to live. Slowly, he found a place to live with only the clothes on his back. He started prostituting to make money for food, rent, and clothing. The experience of men using him sexually was the first time he really experienced a man touching him in what seemed like a loving way. He never finished high school, but he learned how to obtain jobs and survive.

Now, is it possible that Andrew may never recover from these wounds, this relational damage? I think it's very possible that he may always live with some of the emotional scars. The impact this damage has upon him may never fully disappear. Having same-sex attractions, which Andrew did, may always be with him because full restoration and healing of his heart and soul will never happen on earth. However, one day Andrew's full healing *will* take place! One day he *will* be fully changed with no more struggles with sexual attractions for the same sex.

I share Andrew's story not to communicate the idea that everyone with same-sex attractions has a horrific life. Some of us have much milder forms of damage. My own story does not match many of the men I have counseled. Whereas a number of men I have counseled have been treated much more horribly than I was, I grew up in a fairly healthy and calm environment. There was no sexual, physical, emotional, or spiritual abuse in my home. My mother and father remained married until their deaths much later in life. We had food, clothing, and shelter. I do not recall a time of ever going without basic necessities.

So if my home was a healthy place, what could possibly have happened that led to my having same-sex attractions? I will answer this question in the next chapter.

5

The Way Life Should Be

IN PREVIOUS CHAPTERS WE developed an understanding of what we need as people, and what happens when traumas occur and we don't bring resolution to our pain. In order to work through traumas, it's important to look at our lives like a puzzle. There are many pieces, and until you look at every piece, you only complete part of the story. The goal in walking through the puzzle pieces of our lives is not necessarily to experience an internal or external change. The goal is to see the whole picture, face the reality of our lives, discover the wounds, and then find healing and resolution. As we each walk this path, changes naturally occur which may lead to relational health.

The degree that individuals experience transformation is contingent on the amount of emotional damage, combined with their willingness to examine each piece of the puzzle of their life and work with what they've been given.

PARENTAL RELATIONSHIPS

Some may react strongly to the concept of parents' having an influence on one's sexual identity. I acknowledge that poor parental relationship does not *cause* same-sex attraction. At the same time, an equally inaccurate and imbalanced perspective would say that relationships with our parents don't impact us *at all* in terms of our sexual identity. Parents are the very first humans with whom we connect relationally. They have a huge impact upon the foundation of what we believe, how we feel about ourselves, how we relate to the world, our understanding of what it means to be male and female, etc. We cannot dismiss the significance of these relationships.

Author and speaker Brené Brown, who has done research on the issue of shame and vulnerability, stated in her recent book *Daring Greatly*: "I have no doubt, however, that when it comes to our sense of love, belonging, and worthiness, we are most radically shaped by our families of origin—what we hear, what we are told, and perhaps most importantly, how we observe our parents engaging with the world."[1]

In addition, she talks about the specific experience of hope and how it is linked with parental relationships: "Hope is learned! According to [C.R. Snyder's research on hope], children most often learn hope from their parents. To learn hopefulness, children need relationships that are characterized by boundaries, consistency, and support. Children with high levels of hopefulness have experience with adversity. They've been given the opportunity to struggle and in doing that they learn how to believe in themselves."[2]

To develop a mature approach, we need to avoid blaming people. The more mature perspective is to see how we are impacted by those in our lives and examine how we have responded to that impact.

According to Scripture, another issue we face is that we are slaves to sin apart from Christ. We are born with a sinful nature. Paul explains this in one of his epistles in the New Testament:

> So the trouble is not with the law, for it is spiritual and good. The trouble is with me, for I am all too human, a slave to sin. I don't really understand myself, for I want to do what is right, but I don't do it. Instead, I do what I hate. But if I know that what I am doing is wrong, this shows that I agree that the law is good. So I am not the one doing wrong; it is sin living in me that does it. (Rom. 7:14–17)

We are immature and sinful in how we respond to our experiences. We can't help but do the opposite of what God desires in how we live and respond to life. In order to overcome our sinful nature, we need to have Christ residing in us, which is part of the reason for his death on the cross. Through his death and resurrection, Jesus Christ brought victory over sin and death (Rom. 8:1–14).

---

1. Brown, *Daring Greatly*, 217.
2. Ibid., 240.

The reality that we are impacted by our parents is only one part of the equation in our relationships with them. We must be cognizant of our sinful nature and how it impacts us before we have a relationship with Christ.

THE IDEAL

God intended that, from the time we are born, we would have both a mother and father who take care of us. They meet not only our physical needs—food, clothing, shelter, and medical care—but they also meet our emotional and spiritual needs. As we enter the world, parents are not only our first examples of human relationships; they are also our first examples of what it means to be male and female. In addition, they model what it is to have a relationship with God. We are too immature as infants, toddlers, and preschoolers to have a concept of relating to a being that we cannot see, hear, or feel much of the time. Our parents represent that tangible relationship as well, preparing us by laying the foundation of a relationship with God in the future. There is a lot going on in our relationship with our parents, especially during the first five years of life before we enter school.

As we look at parental behavior, though, let me remind you not to jump to conclusions and believe that your parents caused your problems today. Unless they are standing over you, beating you with a bat, we need to be very cognizant that as a young adult or adult we are more fully responsible for our behavior than when we were children. The goal in looking at our relationships with our parents is to identify how we've been impacted and evaluate how we have chosen to respond to that impact. This process sets us up for the problems we face as adolescents, young adults, and adults.

We've already looked at the value of Type A needs within all of us. In order for us to grow up and be mature as adults, we need to have our Type A needs met, which results in our feeling *secure and valued, and gives us an understanding of gender identity*. Gender identity is not something we are left to ourselves to develop. We need guidance there as well. Developing security, value, and gender identity are the primary tasks of parents.

Accomplishing this goal is quite challenging. As I always teach parents, it doesn't take any work to be a poor or bad parent. That comes naturally. But it takes a ton of work to be a good or healthy parent.

To develop security in a child, numbers 5 and 6 (age-appropriate limits and basic needs met) on the Type A list need to be present, particularly for the first twelve years. Continually providing the physical needs of a child and having healthy discipline (setting age-appropriate limits) enable the child to believe that he or she can rely upon the parents to provide what is needed for any ache, pain, or desire. If certain needs aren't met, there is an assurance from the parents that they are aware of the needs and desires, and an explanation for why they can't be met at that time.

One day, when my older son, Micah, was around six years old, he was on the first floor of our home. He called out for me, as I was on the second floor helping my younger son get dressed for the day. "Daddy?" he called.

My younger son Noah responded, "What?"

Then Micah replied, "No, Noah, you're not daddy. You don't take care of us."

You see, by age six, Micah already had a belief system that daddies take care of their children. There was no fear or insecurity in his voice. My continuing to provide these basic needs is imperative to ensuring that Micah and Noah have security in this world.

With regard to developing value in a child, numbers 1–4, 7, and 8 are key. (See chapter 2.) Initially, parents are the exclusive sources for enabling a child to feel valued. The authors of *Living from the Heart Jesus Gave You* state in their book that every infant needs to have the experience of being a "sparkle in someone's eye."[3] They explain how experiencing joy is an important part of our development in the early years, not only emotionally but physiologically as well.

> Having enough joy strength is fundamental to a person's well-being. We now know that a "joy center" exists in the right orbital prefrontal cortex of the brain. It has executive control over the entire emotional system. When the joy center has been sufficiently developed, it regulates emotions, pain control, and immunity centers; it guides us to act like ourselves; it releases neurotransmitters like dopamine and serotonin; and it is the only part of the brain that overrides the main drive centers—food and sexual impulses, terror and rage.[4]

THE EARLY YEARS: LAYING THE FOUNDATION

Let's break down this development even more. When it comes to security in the early years, the mother is more important for a child. The father is

3. Friesen et al., *Living From the Heart Jesus Gave You*, 20.

4. Ibid., 12.

not unimportant, but the initial relationship tends to be with mother, since she is the one who primarily feeds the infant through breast-feeding. In her womb and in her breasts, mother lays the foundation for security and for the child to trust.

Psalm 22:9 states, "Yet you brought me safely from my mother's womb and led me to trust you at my mother's breast." Not only does this verse support the idea of trust developing in a mother's womb and at the breast, but also that this trust is directly connected with developing trust with God later in life. Babies are very important people and much is going on in their little hearts and minds, whether we can see it or not.

With regard to identity, babies see themselves merely as an extension of their mothers. They don't differentiate from her until they develop an understanding of object permanence. This allows children to see themselves as separate from an object. Child development experts like to use an experiment that involves placing a ball under a blanket. A child that doesn't understand object permanence yet will look around, wondering what happened to the ball. A child who recognizes object permanence will pull the blanket away, knowing that the ball didn't disappear. It was just covered up. When a baby gains mobility through crawling and walking, that child is then prepared to start seeing him- or herself as separate and different from mother.

In males, the earliest signs of separating from mother and starting to connect with father take place around eighteen months of age. As a young toddler boy moves toward daddy, he needs to be in a safe and welcoming place.

Dr. Melvin Wong is a Christian psychologist who has researched basic human development and applied this to individuals who have unwanted same-sex attractions. Several years ago, he gave a talk at a conference I attended in Toronto, Canada, explaining this important developmental step in boys. When I first heard this talk, my wife and I were actually going through this step with our younger son, Noah, not knowing what was really going on. My wife and I spent equal time taking care of our boys each day. When we were both present on weekends, we noticed that the boys would often go to her first when they needed something, even though I was also faithful to provide their needs during the week.

However, at eighteen months of age, they suddenly started coming to me when both my wife and I were present. Sometimes even mid-walk, our sons would shift from going toward her and approach me instead. We would look at each other and ask, "What just happened?"

This shift is what Dr. Wong was talking about when he explained the early beginnings of a young boy seeking to connect with the masculine. So much of what happens in our lives starts at a very early age, even at what we in ministry call pre-memory stage. We cannot avoid looking at this part of life because it does impact our growth and development. It is important to remember the foundation for relational connection with both males and females is being laid in the early years.

Those who argue against environmental explanations for same-sex attraction often don't value the early stages in a child's life and dismiss it simply because they can't remember it. Their parents may not be able to report the significance of what took place in their lives. However, sometimes experiences and insights are revealed that give us clear understanding.

Let me share an example. There was once a tall white man who regularly attended a support group I led. He shared at one point that he didn't like people touching him. The only type of people he didn't mind touching him were big African American women. This was rather unusual, and he was always uncertain as to why this was so. During the course of the support group, he shared one night how he had a conversation with his parents about his life. They said to each other, "Remember when he almost died?"

He yelled out, "What? I almost died?"

His parents then proceeded to explain that when he was only a few months old, he became very ill and had to be hospitalized. At that time, parents weren't allowed to be in the same room with their child when he or she was very ill. At this hospital, a big, African American woman would walk around, holding him and singing to him in the nursery.

What happened? The separation from his parents that this man experienced as a baby was very traumatic. He was very ill and needed to have comfort from his mother and father. They were prevented from being with him, so he detached emotionally from them in his pain. This was the only way he could handle the trauma. He then reattached to the African American woman who was his comfort and security. Isn't this amazing? Through a traumatic experience, God provided, but it impacted how he related to people well into his adulthood.

In this case, there was no blame to be placed upon the parents or the infant. If there was any fault, the blame would probably exclusively be on the medical community for not valuing the parent-infant relationship. This separation impacted this man in such a way that, as an adult, he didn't function normally when it came to receiving physical affection. When this memory was shared with him, by God's grace, he was able to take it and we were able to pray through it. He could understand himself better and move toward receiving affection from others in healthy ways.

This is a great example of the significance of what happens to us even in our infancy. We can't always know everything that impacts us. We are completely dependent upon God, who knows our days intimately, to reveal these things to us.

Those who stand against environmental explanations for same-sex attractions need to be willing to admit that they don't know everything. This lack of knowledge could actually be the key to explaining significant behavior, feelings, and beliefs in a person, even for those with same-sex attractions. We need to be willing to live with mystery and let God reveal to us what we need to know. Following his standards for relationship and sexuality is important. We can then trust him to explain what we don't understand because we trust and believe that he knows what's best.

GRADE SCHOOL YEARS: BUILDING THE STRUCTURE

As children grow and develop between six to twelve years of age, one way that parents show love and support is to understand and know their likes and desires. As children develop areas of interests, parents provide opportunities to experiment with these different activities. They help them distinguish between mere interest and a true passion that can grow and develop. The parents then help them grow in that area of passion, not to affirm their own identity, but to help their children understand that part of their identity. They help them see that the activity does not define who they are, but who they are can be expressed better through these various activities and opportunities.

We have often gotten this wrong in raising children. Activities and talents should never be where children or parents get their value and identity. Value and worth is in the child's existence, and that identity is totally tied to the fact that he or she is created by God. Once children have put their faith in Christ, their identities remain as sons or daughters for the remainder of life. Any talent, gift, or ability is merely an expression of the uniqueness of that child—not anything that proves his or her worth and value.

It is a common problem in our culture for children to be pushed too early into sports or art and music. An immature culture raises adults who, out of their insecurity, are tempted to look to their children to find their own value and identity. That's why many parents can come across as controlling of a child's behavior. They are trying to shape and mold the child in a way that places a positive view on the parent.

With regard to gender identity, parents model for the child what it means to be a male and female. Healthy men and women don't restrict children to cultural views of masculinity and femininity, which are often broken and inaccurate. They are able to model more biblical views on these aspects of gender, which we will address later in another chapter. For now, it's just important to know that the foundation for gender relies upon the parents' modeling for the children.

During the grade school years (ages six to twelve), understanding gender becomes more challenging. The child is exposed to other children in school. At school, broken views of what it means to be a boy or girl are modeled all the time. Children are often shamed for being the opposite gender when they model behaviors that are outside the bounds of what the culture might determine as masculine or feminine. That's why terms like *sissy* or *tomboy* have often been used in recent American history. These terms were used to describe boys and girls in a negative light rather than edifying their uniqueness and allowing room for variation in gender. Even though adults can be guilty of using these terms, boys and girls are often merciless in using such terms.

Part of the job of the parent, though, is to help the child sift through the broken views expressed outside the home. As the son or daughter come home and express confusion and frustration, and pain and hurt regarding gender, parents can correct these views and affirm the uniqueness of the child.

My son Micah started to face this struggle in third grade. A number of factors were going on then, but we noticed that he started to speak negatively of boys and state that he didn't like boys or sports. One thing I have always loved about Micah is that whatever is on his mind comes out of his mouth. This can get him into trouble at times, but I love that you know where he stands. You know what he's feeling. This makes it possible for me to know, without much effort, what is going on in his heart.

One night at the dinner table, Micah said, "Noah is a *real* boy, but not me." My wife and I asked what he meant. He stated that Noah likes to play sports and gets along with the other boys. But he likes to go shopping and doesn't get along with boys.

Micah's observations perfectly exemplify being a great observer but poor interpreter. He has observed carefully how his brother relates to boys and how they respond to him. Then he assesses his own interactions with boys. However, his conclusion is that *he* is not a boy.

At this point, it is absolutely necessary for me as a parent to correct his thinking and actively affirm his masculinity during the normal course of life. This also calls me to evaluate my own definitions of masculinity and correct any false views within my own mind and heart.

Fortunately I had already done a lot of work in the area of masculinity in my own life. My definition differed from that of the American culture. At that time, my wife and I were able to explain that masculinity was not restricted to liking sports and getting along with other boys. We not only spoke of how boys and men can look different, but we also began implementing some new activities in Micah's life. We started inviting other boys to come over and spend time playing with him one-on-one.

When boys get into a group, in their immaturity they will gravitate toward the stronger personalities and the gender behavior exhibited by those individuals. Getting a boy alone with another boy breaks down those barriers and misperceptions, and they are more likely to be themselves. Micah began to find out that he was not so different from other boys.

In addition, we got Micah into a sport that was more individualized than team-focused. Teams can be intimidating for Micah, but individualized sports are more conducive to his working out insecurities about sports. So, fencing became his sport for several years, and he became quite good at it and won some medals at competitions. He changed his perception that he was no longer good at sports, and he became confident enough to experiment with the team sports that he normally avoided.

What my wife and I did was part of what it means to be a parent. We needed to know how our child feels and the lies he believes, and to help him correct those lies so he could view himself and the world around him correctly. We also needed to be proactive about his activities and use them to help him work through false perceptions.

Honestly, being a parent in this manner is way more work. It would be much easier to sit on the couch and watch TV, and I certainly have been tempted to do this. Sometimes I *have* just sat and watched TV and checked out. But this would not help my sons grow into the men I know they can become.

ADOLESCENCE: COMPLETION OF THE STRUCTURE

As children enter adolescence, many changes take place. Security is established in a child when the parents have consistently provided food, clothing, shelter, and medical care. There is little concern, if any, about having basic physical needs provided.

With regard to gender, the body explodes with hormones that start influencing the desires children have for the opposite sex. For males, testosterone increases by 500 percent during adolescence. It's no wonder our heads don't blow off during that time!

God planned that children would grow up in healthy homes. A natural result of healthy development is that a child will be drawn toward the opposite sex.

The question of what causes heterosexuality has been brought up. The truth is that we will naturally be heterosexual if we grow up in healthy environments because this is how God created humans to function. We are meant to enter a home with a mother and father who love us well. Then we proceed to develop healthy connections with same-sex peers. Healthy connections with peers help solidify healthy perceptions of the masculine and feminine. Boys are affirmed and girls are affirmed, both inside and outside the home. Once there is security in one's gender, then there is freedom to be drawn to and step out toward the opposite sex. Opposite-sex relationships are more complicated and challenging for humans, and thus maturity is required to enter them. This is the normal progression that God intended for all humans.

The reason this development doesn't take place is because we have sinful natures, people sin against us, and we have an enemy seeking to destroy anything that edifies the image of God. Men and women were created in the image of God to reflect who he is, and the marriage relationship is the perfect complementarity of relationships to accurately reflect God. Satan will do anything to tarnish this image, and a great way to do this is to confuse people in their gender.

In healthy adolescence, though, males and females move toward each other. Since they still aren't mature, they will make mistakes and be awkward with each other. Parents can continue to help their children work through these trials and errors in relationships with the opposite sex.

The father becomes more important for both genders at this stage. For males, father helps son to step out in his uniqueness as a male and blesses him. He can be a cheerleader for his son, helping him through mistakes and sending him back out to successfully pursue a female. For females, the father calls his daughter out as unique from her mother. During adolescence, conflict increases between mother and daughter because the daughter wants to become her own person. The father helps to buffer the conflict and blesses his daughter, calling her beautiful in her own person. He also models for her what kind of character she should be looking for in a man.

With regard to value, adolescents who have grown up in a healthy home will know that they are valued and loved by their parents. They've had over twelve years of both parents' affirming, giving physical affection, and time spent supporting activities important to the children. Now the adolescents want to know that someone outside the family will pick them. They think, "I know my mom and dad love me. I want to know that someone who is not familiar with me will also like and value me." This is why adolescents look to peers to gain affirmation. They want to know that people in the world will want to be with them and choose them as a friend.

Being pursued and being chosen is an important part of feeling valued in the world. Adolescence can be a painful time because not being chosen and not being pursued can hurt. Once children are pursued and chosen as friends, and then eventually as spouses, there is further evidence for their value and worth.

THE PROBLEM OF SIN

I have explained a lot of the ideal that God intended for us as humans. We have one problem, though: sin entered the world with Adam and Eve. Ever since then, we as human beings battle our fleshly, sinful nature. A natural consequence of our sinful nature is that we damage relationships.

I want to give you a definition of sin that I learned from Dan Allender, a Christian counselor and author, at one of his conferences a long time ago. Prior to this, no one had ever given me a definition of sin.

When I was a recent college graduate, I went on a mission trip to Japan in hopes of sharing Jesus Christ with Japanese college students. We were trained in Tokyo before traveling to Nagoya for the summer. During the training, we were taught about how the concept of sin can be confusing for the Japanese. We needed to spend time learning how to explain what we meant when we used that term.

I think we are in the same situation in the United States. Sin is a very confusing word and its general meaning has been lost. When I've asked what sin is during many speaking engagements, a common answer is "Sin is what God says is wrong."

Well, yes . . . But why would he say something is wrong? I think it's all right to consider that God has reasons for why he states something is sin. If we are going to talk about sin, then we need to have an agreed-upon understanding.

Dan Allender gave this definition of sin and I have used it ever since: "Sin is anything that damages or destroys relationship with God and/or people."

Let's use this definition when talking about the Law. The Ten Commandments were given to the people of Israel through Moses. Many of you are familiar with these commandments, so let's look at a couple of them. "You must not steal" is the eighth commandment (Ex. 20:15). Why? You can't really love someone well if you are stealing from him or her. Stealing from someone is not the way to love your friend, family member, or neighbor.

"You must not commit murder" is the seventh commandment (Ex. 20:13). Why? Murder *ends* relationship. You can't have relationship with someone who is dead. In addition, you have destroyed something God has created, a human that's been created in his image. You are damaging your relationship with God by declaring that his creation is garbage and not worth living.

Whenever I look at anything God says is sin in the Bible, I go back to this definition and see how the behavior damages relationships. When it comes to sexual sin, all sexual sin damages relationship, even if we don't fully understand how. We are working with God's definition of sin, not yours and mine. We are working with God's definition of love, not yours and mine. Americans have a very immature view of love, and we need a holy God to help us understand what true love is.

Since sin entered the world, relationships are continually damaged in a myriad of ways. Sometimes the damage is great and sometimes the damage is minor. When we talk about parental relationships, parents can never be perfect because they face the same battle that you, I, and every human being on earth face. We *all* battle sin in our lives.

Paul makes that clear when he says, "All have sinned and fall short of the glory of God" (Rom. 3:23). We need the Holy Spirit within us to even have the desire to live as God wants us to live in relationship with him and people. For Christians, the Spirit is helping us live differently but we still fail in the process of giving up our flesh in exchange for the Spirit's desires. As Christian parents, we still damage our children in relationship because we aren't perfect yet. For those who don't have Christ, we have already addressed the fact that they are slaves to sin. The potential for damaging relationship is even greater because they can't overcome any sin without the power of the Holy Spirit within them.

This developmental process contributes to the foundation laid for developing same-sex attractions. Remember to keep the perspective that parents do not *cause* same-sex attractions, but they do impact children in a way that contributes to the development of these desires.

6

The Drive for Completion

ANOTHER IMPORTANT ASPECT OF normal development is that we need to be able to connect relationally with peers of the same sex. Bullying is a hot issue in our culture today, with much effort being made to diminish the impact of bullying, if not to eliminate this hostile behavior altogether.

However, bullying is not the only action that impacts a child's heart. Abuse is definitely a trauma, but not being cherished, not being seen as valuable simply by virtue of one's existence, is another trauma. If a child's value is not communicated at home, then the next place to go is outside the home to find that value.

Dr. Joseph Nicolosi and his wife, Linda, write about this important developmental step of same-sex friendships. Dr. Nicolosi is an expert on the development of same-sex attractions in males. In their book *A Parent's Guide to Preventing Homosexuality*, they focus more specifically on a boy's development:

> You should always remember that besides your immediate family, same-sex peers are among the most important influences in your son's life. Male friends are key factors in masculine gender formation and future heterosexual development. The influence of male friendships is illustrated by a particularly intriguing study that found that even for nursery-school boys, their male classmates had a stronger influence on them than did their adult teachers. Clinician Richard Friedman also found male friendships to be frequently painfully distorted during the juvenile phase of childhood

in homosexual males. Dr. Friedman believes that isolation from other boys plays a central role in homosexual development.[1]

Is the same true in the development of girls? Janelle Hallman is a licensed professional counselor who specializes in female homosexuality and emotional dependencies. In her book *The Heart of Female Same-Sex Attraction,* she states:

> Nevertheless, to become ultimately secure in their girlhood or feminine identity, these girls at least needed to discover and identify with some desirable and respectable characteristics and traits within some women or social images of females. If a gender-nonconforming girl finds other females who enjoy the same thing she enjoys and if she receives ongoing acceptance, respect, and affirmation as a girl, all may be well. A girl can still proceed to develop a healthy sense of femaleness and femininity.[2]

Without developing healthy same-sex friendships in childhood, the child will respond in ways that will set him or her up for varying kinds of problems or struggles in the future. Contrary to God's original plan, many children do not feel very connected with the same sex and often develop broken ideas of what it means to be male or female. Again, I am not saying that poor same-sex friendships *cause* same-sex attractions. However, a lack of same-sex friendships is one component in the development of homosexual struggles.

When it comes to my story, I want to clarify that I wasn't attracted to just any man. This is a common misunderstanding among those who've never had same-sex attractions. Just because someone has same-sex attraction doesn't mean one is attracted to *anyone* who is in the same-sex category. There are what the American culture might call *preferences.* What I have come to understand is that our specific attractions are influenced by the ways we are impacted relationally and how we suppress our emotions.

1. Nicolosi and Nicolosi, *A Parent's Guide to Preventing Homosexuality,* 95. Research cited from Fagot, "Beyond the Reinforcement Principle," 1097–104; and Friedman, *Male Homosexuality,* chapter 5.

2. Hallman, *The Heart of Female Same-Sex Attraction,* 77.

EXPLANATION OF VARIATION IN SAME-SEX ATTRACTIONS

I was never attracted to any male that wasn't white. Why was this the case? Does this mean I'm racist?

The rejection I felt from my father was not only rejection from a man, but a man who is Caucasian. My experience with my white male peers was very similar to my experience with my father. My definition of what it meant to be a male was being cold, unfeeling, aggressive, and bullying. Why? Because the male peers at school modeled this type of behavior on a daily basis. If a boy had feelings of any kind that weren't in the category of happiness or anger, then that boy would be called a sissy. When I was young, boys were not seen as healthy or strong if they cried. Crying was a negative behavior for males, and to feel insecure in any way was a sign of weakness.

When I was growing up, my experience with any males who were not white was minimal. There were *no* non-white males in my grade school. I was in a small, rural community and very few non-whites lived in the town at all.

My family moved to a larger city when I was around twelve, and the population of non-whites was significantly larger than in the small town I came from. There was one African American male in my middle school, in the same grade as I. The other males, who were white, were the ones who consistently beat me up and made fun of me, calling me "sissy" and "fag." I was starting to become attracted to males in middle school, and it freaked me out that they knew how I was feeling without my saying a word!

I was confused. Maybe there were unwritten rules as to what was male and what was not male. They all seemed to know what the rules were, but not I. Why didn't anyone tell me about these rules? I would have followed them if doing so could get me out of all this abuse.

But the abuse wasn't coming from the African American kid, who happened to be popular. He was a good athlete and everyone loved him. No one made fun of him or mocked him. He fit in the category of the athletic, popular guy. However, he never made fun of me, even when the other males around him were. He would look at me but it was more with a look of pity rather than one of mockery. Now I was definitely confused. I came to a poor interpretation: Being white and male is a bad thing! Being black and male is a good thing!

My experiences with non-white males continued to be positive. White males were the source of all my pain both at home and outside the home. I felt unseen and unloved by anyone who was a white male. My definition of masculinity and perception of males were all related to being white. My rejection of my father and my male peers, who were all white, was suppressed deep within. My deep desires were to be connected with my father and with male peers. Since I'm white, I especially wanted to feel included among white males. So when I rejected males, I also rejected the "whiteness" that was part of the masculine definition. Suppressed desires bubble up and that longing for men, and white males in particular, became sexual.

Other men I have known are white and are only attracted to African American males. Some Asian males have been attracted only to white males. Again, these specific attractions are not preferences but ways that particular suppressed desires bubble up. What is emphasized is the rejection of masculinity as a whole, and if that includes race, it will be thrown in the mix as well.

Repeating what we've mentioned earlier, your behavior tells the truth about yourself, not what you believe or say—unless they happen to match. The behavior of having specific sexual attractions is always a reflection of what's going on deep within one's heart. The same is actually true for heterosexuals, but our focus of this book is on same-sex attraction, so this is where we will continue our explanation.

SEEKING COMPLETION IN THE SAME SEX

Being around boys was intimidating for me. I didn't seem to carry around the self-confidence that many of them had. I understand now that the insecurities I felt at home, with a father that related to me in a confusing manner, transferred to my relating with male peers in school.

Having close friendships with same-sex peers is another important developmental step. Without this step being completed well, one cannot grow up to be a healthy person. Boys need to have good relational connections with other males. This is imperative. Our immature American culture values relationships so little that minimal guidance is given on how to have good relationships. Our fathers typically didn't learn how to have good male friendships growing up, so they had little to pass on to their sons. They settled for less in the realm of friendships. As children, we then live out an immature perspective on friendship. This ends up feeling less and less satisfying, which, in turn, results in our giving up on friendships and suppressing those desires for a "bosom buddy."

Most men who have same-sex attractions have the same experience of not feeling connected with male peers as children. Most women with same-sex attractions felt disconnected from females as children and thought they didn't fit the stereotype of what a female should be. What men and women with same-sex attractions are looking for in relationships is not necessarily what others observe, or even what that person thinks. What they desire, initially, is to be in a relationship with someone of the same sex. That's how their desires are manifested, but often the deeper desire is buried and ignored. The deeper desires are often unseen or unknown, not just by gays and lesbians but by heterosexuals as well. However, some people have been able to identify these deeper desires as they have investigated what's really inside their hearts.

Tim Timmerman, a professor of art at George Fox University, wrote an amazing and underrated book called *A Bigger World Yet*. Tim shares his own struggles with same-sex attraction and conversations with others who have struggled or identified as gay. He has also studied male friendships throughout history. He recounts what a friend once told him: "I was looking for something that I didn't see in myself. I was looking for power, I was looking for masculinity, I was looking for confidence and connection to men, and I didn't know how to get it other than sexuality. It's all I was looking for; it was never about sex. It was about connection and finding in others, looking to others for the things I didn't see in myself."[3]

Tim's friend was willing to be honest and address the deeper issues of his heart. Leanne Payne, a leader in the healing prayer movement, wrote a book called *The Broken Image*. In this book, she teaches about counseling individuals with same-sex attractions, and she identifies what she learned during times of counseling and prayer. She explains what she calls the *cannibal compulsion* as being a part of the experience of same-sex attraction. "Do you know anything at all about the habits of cannibals? Do you know why they eat people? . . . I told him what a missionary once told me: 'Cannibals eat only those they admire, and they eat them to get their traits.'

3. Timmerman, *A Bigger World Yet*, 57.

What was happening to Matthew was very clear: he was looking at the other young man and loving a lost part of himself; a part that he could not recognize or accept."[4] This is particularly true of a failure to recognize and accept one's own gender identity.

Leanne Payne had an impact on Andy Comiskey's story. He himself came out of homosexuality and started "a healing/support group in West Hollywood, California, for men and women seeking Jesus in light of unwanted same-sex attractions."[5] He clarifies what Leanne Payne means by cannibal compulsion: "Cannibal compulsion is grounded in legitimate needs for same-sex intimacy and for gender integration. Its expression is legitimate, however, as it is a man-made fallen attempt to find love and wholeness. As such, cannibal compulsion leads to idolatry. Any attempt to set up a member of one's own sex as the completion of one's adult sexuality is a lie. God's creative intent for all is the freedom to emerge into the freedom of whole, heterosexual relating."[6]

COMPLETION IN CHRIST ALONE

This behavior is considered idolatry because it is our attempt, as human beings, to solve our own problems and struggles apart from God. We put faith in a human being to complete us rather than God.

Those with same-sex attractions are not the only ones that practice this cannibal compulsion. Heterosexuals can do the very same thing by putting their faith and trust in the opposite sex to complete them where they lack. A famous example is in the movie *Jerry Maguire* in which the main character says to his wife, Dorothy, *"You complete me."* The lie is that a human being can complete you.

There is value in how opposite sexes complement one another in relationship, but the opposite sex is never meant to fill what only God can fill. This is the same for same-sex relationships as well. In fact, in Colossians 2 Paul specifically states, "For in Christ lives all the fullness of God in a human body. So you also are complete through your union with Christ, who is the head over every ruler and authority" (vv. 9–10).

Our completion is meant to be in Christ, not a person. Christ has everything we need, even though it can be difficult sometimes to see how.

4. Payne, *The Broken Image*, 46–47.

5. Desert Stream/Living Waters Ministries, "History," lines 1–2.

6. Comiskey, *Living Waters Support Group Manual*, 110.

Now, I think it's important to know that men and women don't consciously choose to be "cannibalistic" in their actions. The process is a subconscious behavior that has to be brought to light. Again, our behavior tells the truth about us, and looking at our behavior helps identify what is underlying the behavior. In the case of cannibal compulsion, the sexual or romantic behavior is an attempt to complete what the person feels is lacking in terms of masculinity or femininity.

Many of the men I have counseled have often expressed they weren't looking for sex but for a man to just hold them, to show affection and affirmation. When asked what they feel they are lacking in themselves in terms of feeling masculine, the traits they express often match what they are attracted to in another man. I've seen the same kind of experience among women with same-sex attraction that I have counseled. Sometimes the traits are reflected in physical traits, and sometimes they are emotional or character traits.

I was attracted to men who were muscular, athletic, and had chest hair. My belief was that my own body, lacking in muscles and hair, reflected my lack of masculine traits. Therefore, I was not *really* a man. Being attracted to these types of men was my attempt to connect with those who had what I lacked, thus completing me and helping me feel masculine once again.

These men would have been less of a draw to me had I been securely attached to my father and had some sense of connection to the masculine. My strong desire for connecting with males outside of my home was influenced by my lack of connection with the masculine in my home. When I was with the types of men I just described, I would feel secure with myself. If they didn't accept or approve of me, then I would sit in insecurity, not feeling content with who I was or how God made me.

I want to remind you that the realities I have explained do not *cause* same-sex attractions. However, what we experience in terms of connecting well with the same sex has an impact on our souls, which in turn impacts the kind of struggles we have. The main issue to remember is that we often suppress what is in the depths of our hearts. We can have a completely different thought process in our minds, but our behavior is influenced by the beliefs and feelings in our hearts. That's why someone can be driving to an adult bookstore or going online to look at porn while thinking, "I shouldn't be doing this."

We can believe we are secure in our masculinity or femininity, but if our behavior doesn't match this belief, then we are unaware of the beliefs within our hearts that need to be revealed. Sometimes these beliefs can be revealed through asking questions and talking freely without any hindrances; other times they are revealed through times of healing prayer. Stressful moments or having conflict in relationships or prolonged periods of suffering also can reveal deep belief systems within. Pain has a way of surfacing things in ways that times of ease cannot do. I have a much easier time ignoring my heart when my circumstances are fine, as compared to when I am challenged and pushed in ways that stir up painful feelings within.

WHAT JESUS DID DO

I think Jesus' approach to living life as a human on earth is very fascinating. He could have chosen any method to travel around and proclaim his lordship. He could have stayed an isolated loner, speaking from the tops of hills, looking down on everyone, and remaining distant. However, he chose to be up close and personal. He spent three years with his disciples, eating, sleeping, walking, talking, and ministering together. They had intimate conversations on a daily basis. The disciples argued and Jesus refereed.

Jesus wasn't just living this method for himself alone. I believe part of his motivation for living as he did was to model what it is like to follow God and impart truth to those who are less mature. Discipling someone cannot be a mere intellectual project. With Jesus, there is a come-and-see, come-and-do approach. No longer is there distance in our relationship with God. He's right here in flesh and blood and yet still God. After Jesus ascended into heaven, the Holy Spirit descends and resides within believers, once again bringing relationship with God up close and personal.

When the early church formed, people started living in community, sharing all their resources with each other, and no one was left in need of anything (Acts 2:42–47; 4:32–35). Life was no longer about everyone fighting for self, trying to obtain food and clothing on a penny's income. Jesus spoke to the disciples about a *new* way of living when he said, "So now I am giving you a new commandment: Love each other. Just as I have loved you, you should love each other. Your love for one another will prove to the world that you are my disciples" (John 13:34–35).

Now the followers of Jesus live life in a new way, separate from the world. Believers help one another and are responsible for one another. Jesus didn't just make this statement; he *lived* this way of life with his disciples.

That's why he stated *as I have loved you.* Jesus was for real, living out the truth with his behavior, his life.

Paul carries Jesus' perspective further in Philippians 2: "Is there any encouragement from belonging to Christ? Any comfort from his love? Any fellowship together in the Spirit? Are your hearts tender and compassionate? Then make me truly happy by agreeing wholeheartedly with each other, loving one another, and working together with one mind and purpose. Don't be selfish; don't try to impress others. Be humble, thinking of others as better than yourselves. Don't look out only for your own interests, but take an interest in others, too" (vv. 1–4).

I always love reading Christian books about what it means to be male or female because so few well-written ones exist. I recently read a great Larry Crabb book on masculinity and femininity called *Fully Alive.* This book is well worth reading. He addresses this passage in the book but makes a correction to the translation of verse 4. Here is what he says:

> Paul seems to be saying, "Look out for yourself but also look out for others." However, according to reputable Bible scholars who look carefully into the original wording, the word *only* is not there. Delete *only* and *also* is no longer needed. Paul's instruction, then, is this: "Let each of you look not to his own interests, but to the interests of others." The change in meaning is as radical as it is profound, and as profound as it is impossible—without the Holy Spirit. If we are to be spiritually formed into relationally masculine men and feminine women, the *end* of self-centeredness is required, not its socialization. We are to crucify the managed life that aims toward our felt well-being. We are not to live an acceptable blend of self-centeredness and other-centeredness. There is no acceptable blend of hell's virtues with heaven's.[7]

My belief is that part of the reason same-sex attraction has become a growing issue is that it exposes the brokenness of relationships in our culture. Jacqueline Olds and Richard S. Schwartz have written a book called *The Lonely American* that does a beautiful job assessing our American culture. Olds and Schwartz record how sociologist Philip Slater states the following:

> We seek a private house, a private means of transportation, a private garden, a private laundry, self-service stores, and do-it-yourself skills of every kind. An enormous technology seems to

---

7. Crabb, *Fully Alive,* 203–204.

have set itself the task of making it unnecessary for one human being ever to ask anything of another in the course of going about his daily business. Even within the family Americans are unique in their feeling that each member should have a separate room, and even a separate telephone, television, and car when economically possible. We seek more and more privacy, and feel more and more alienated and lonely when we get it.[8]

WAYS THAT AMERICAN BELIEVERS CAN DO AS JESUS DID

Americans are lonely people. We have increasing technology that supposedly connects us more with people, but we still seem to live isolated lives and feel unknown, unseen. *We* as believers need to take ownership of how we have contributed to our cultural ways of relating: keeping our distance from people, isolating ourselves in our own activities, not making other people a priority over our own lives and plans. Instead of living the life that Christ lived, we are more influenced to live in the same way as our non-Christian American friends and neighbors. Instead of considering others' needs over our own, we predominantly take care of ourselves and occasionally reach out to help someone. Christ gave his life for us and he calls us to do the same (Phil. 2:6–11)! What has caused us, as Christians, to lose the vision of how our Savior lived and how he called us to live?

Some of the reasons people with same-sex attraction don't feel welcome in the church is that they may not be married. And they don't see a large portion of the married church population reaching out to them. Singles, in general, have been neglected in the church. Several of my single friends, who have remained single into their fifties, have all stated the same feeling. They feel like second-class citizens in a church full of married people. The biological family has taken priority over the spiritual family and become an idol.

The church needs to repent of placing our needs over others, including our biological families, and learn how to live in a way in which the spiritual family is included in our definition of family. This will challenge some of us because we feel dominated by the needs of our biological families, but this is where we are called to become mature in how we live. We may not know immediately how to make these changes, but that's part of

8. Olds and Schwartz, *The Lonely American*, 3.

our responsibility as believers, to help one another figure out how to live like Jesus with full plates. Maybe we need our brothers and sisters to help us choose better.

When my wife was battling leukemia, she was incapacitated during several months of treatment. She was not allowed to be in public, even to go to church, while she battled having low blood cell counts. She was very vulnerable to illness and could get an infection easily. If she wasn't in the hospital with treatments, she had to go there every day. The treatment was very intense and involved. Facing her illness and treatments was a daily experience for us, but I also had two children and was pastoring a congregation at the time. My boss gave me the freedom to only work half-time rather than full-time, but there was so much to do in taking basic care of my home and children, as well as my wife.

However, the body of Christ was the answer. People at both my wife's job and mine set up a volunteer schedule for driving Laura to the hospital, making meals for us, cleaning our home, taking our boys to events, and providing financial help for the myriad of expenses we had that year. Can you believe that people provided meals for ten months? God took care of us very well during this very difficult year.

I had not received a get-out-of-jail free card; I wasn't exempt from caring for other people. My church was made up of low-income and homeless people. Many of them knew what it was like to suffer regularly with no certainty of relief from their pain. Some of them could really connect with my family and me during this time because we were suffering in ways they understood. One of the homeless men was also battling a chronic form of leukemia. Laura and I were amazed at how a homeless man had to battle cancer without anything, not even a warm bed to call his own. Being there for other people continued for me, even when my own life was rife with pain and struggles.

I share this to encourage you to see that, if you are willing, God will show you how to give to others even in the most difficult of circumstances in your own life. There may be times in our lives when we have nothing to give and it's the turn of the body of Christ's to serve you. Sometimes loving others means letting them serve you!

Giving to others, however, was not something from which I was exempt while my wife was battling cancer. What I experienced was that God provided me with all the emotional energy I needed to face both my own problems and the struggles of others in my church and the support group I led.

Some days I didn't give out anything. I needed to be served. Other days, however, it was my turn to give to someone out of my own need. God *is* sufficient! We just have to be willing to trust him and follow him. If you choose to follow him, he will take care of whatever you need (Luke 12:31).

My contention is that if we lived out relationship the way God calls us to, then we will have fewer struggles with things like pornography, substance abuse, depression, anxiety, loneliness, *and* same-sex attraction. Our greatest damage happens through relationships and our greatest healing will take place through relationships—relationship with God and the body of Christ.

Also, loving each other as believers is our greatest tool for making evangelism effective. Jesus said in the gospel of John that our love for one another will *prove* to the world that we belong to him (John 13:35). I think that's a pretty important reason to love each other. The New Testament refers to *one another* a couple dozen more times, calling us to serve one another, love one another, and pray for one another. We are obviously called to live a new way of life—the way Jesus lived.

7

The Mystery of Hate

WE HAVE LOOKED AT how God intended us to grow before sin entered the world. Ever since sin entered the world, relationships have been difficult and contentious. To be healthy in relationship takes a *lot* of work, especially in relation to our biological families.

Most people I know *never* receive any training on how to be a good parent. We work with our own experiences, combined with thoughts of what we think is best for a child, but few receive the training necessary to know what children actually need. Children will mess up your world and mine very quickly. Formulas don't work with people. But because we are naturally immature and drawn toward things opposite of God, we run to formulas to *make people work*.

My undergraduate degree is in human development, a social-psychological approach to working with people. During my years of study, I worked with preschool children in a day care on campus. After graduating from college, I had a lot of experience working as a teacher to infants, toddlers, and preschoolers. I had also worked in two different residential homes for adolescents.

Even with all this experience, becoming a parent was an even greater challenge than I had imagined. I wasn't a parent for too long before realizing I needed a lot more information on how to relate to these little beings called my sons. My heart really goes out to parents. Few receive training like I did, and even *with* training, parenting will be one of the most challenging jobs you ever face.

Every parent fails. There's no such thing as a perfect parent. In the twenty years I have been a parent, I have failed on a regular basis as a father. No parent should hang their head in shame for these failures. In fact, Peter Fonagy, a British psychoanalyst and researcher in the field of attachment, suggests that even the *most sensitive parent accurately tracks with his or her child only about 45–50 percent of the time.*[1]

The biggest problem is not that we fail as parents; the greater problem is that we are often afraid to face our weaknesses and learn from them to live in a healthier way. Also, because of our insecurities, we find it difficult to face our failures to ask forgiveness from our children. What should be a normal process in relational life has become a threatening experience for so many people. My hope is to release parents from walking around in shame and encourage them to live into the balanced perspective each of us have failed and succeeded in parenting. This perspective is important as we address the concept of hatred.

What I am about to describe is something I have learned in my twenty-three years of ministry. Only as we are able to face the traumas of our past and identify our reactions and responses to these traumas will we gain the necessary understanding of same-sex attractions. Hatred is another piece of the puzzle.

HOW HATRED LAYS THE FOUNDATION

Almost two decades ago, I had the privilege of going through a fairly intense sexual-abuse training course taught by Dr. Dan Allender, author of *The Wounded Heart*. Dr. Allender has had years of experience counseling people and his teachings influenced me to completely change how I work with people. I've read almost every book he's written, but this conference on sexual abuse had more impact than probably any of his writings.

During the course of the conference, Allender spoke about some things that caused me to pause. I had come to an understanding about same-sex attractions that made sense to me, but the information he was sharing expanded my way of thinking and laid a different foundation for this kind of struggle. So I spoke with him during a break and asked him for

1. Thompson, *Anatomy of the Soul*, 121.

his thoughts about same-sex attractions. At one moment, he specifically stated that homosexuality is rooted in *hatred of the same sex*. I was completely shocked by this statement because no one had ever communicated this before in books or speaking. The break ended, and I wasn't able to fully hash out what he meant by this statement. But I took it back home and started to work with it. I'm going to share with you what I've come to understand as a result. This is information I have seen consistently supported by those with whom I work.

Hatred of the same sex didn't make sense initially. How could I hate men if I'm sexually attracted to them? Being attracted to them seems like I *love* them. What I learned, though, is that Allender was talking about a biblical definition of love and hatred, not our human definitions. Hatred is not always something that you necessarily *feel*.

What do I mean by this statement? I began looking at the Scriptures and started to see support for the idea that hatred can be present without a person ever actually feeling it. For example, in Matthew 6:24 Jesus stated, "No one can serve two masters. For you will hate one and love the other; you will be devoted to one and despise the other. You cannot serve both God and money."

There are many of us who love money probably more than we should. Again, we are going by God's definition of loving money. There are plenty of Scriptures that talk about how God values the poor and cares for them. One of the responsibilities of Christians is that we are to care for the poor.[2]

What Jesus is saying is that if we love money in any way more than we love God, we are actually expressing *hatred* for him! Very few of us would say we *hate* God. We might think that we aren't relating to him as he desires and that we need to work on this issue. Jesus doesn't soften the blow. He calls it what it is. It is *hatred* to love anything more than God! You and I won't necessarily *feel* hatred in our hearts, but our behavior communicates the truth. Our behavior communicates that we are being hateful, according to Jesus.

Here's another example in Proverbs 26:24–26: "People with hate in their hearts may sound pleasant enough, but don't believe them. Though they pretend to be kind, their hearts are full of all kinds of evil. While their

---

2. Here are just a handful of Scriptures that address how God feels about the poor: Lev. 19:15; Deut. 10:17–19; 1 Sam. 2:7–8; Prov. 14:31, 21:13; Matt. 19:21; Luke 4:18; Acts 10:1–4; and James 1:27.

hatred may be concealed by trickery, it will finally come to light for all to see."

Once again, people can *look* like they are nice on the outside, but this isn't always representative of what's really going on in their hearts. You and I can be very "nice" on the outside but can really hate someone within. Haven't you felt this way sometimes with some people you're around? They may be nice to your face, but you can tell something is not quite right. You don't feel like they are truly enjoying your company.

Solomon, the author of Proverbs, gives an example of what hatred looks like in another verse later in that chapter: "A lying tongue hates its victim" (v. 28).

Wow! Solomon calls lying hatred. How many of you have ever lied? I'm sad to say I have but it's true. Have you ever lied to someone you love? Once again, I'm sad to say it but I have. Solomon is stating that whenever I lie, it's an expression of hatred. Again, this isn't a feeling I'm necessarily having *as* I'm lying, but my behavior tells the truth. It's an expression of hatred for that person to lie to him or her.

Here's one last example in 1 John 4:20–21: "If someone says, 'I love God,' but hates a Christian brother or sister, that person is a liar; for if we don't love people we can see, how can we love God, whom we cannot see? And he has given us this command: those who love God must also love their Christian brothers and sisters."

The implication in this verse is that if we say we *hate* a Christian brother or sister, then we are really saying that we *hate* God too! John clearly states that if we can't love people, then we can't possibly love God. And if we don't love God, we hate him. There is no in-between. Jesus doesn't give an in-between with regard to loving God or money, and John does not give us an in-between state either.

All of these verses and explanations are given to help you understand that hate is present in our lives much more than we realize. We like to protect ourselves from the idea that we hate because we don't want to think we are *that* bad. However, the Scriptures state that apart from Christ, we are "desperately wicked and deceitful above all things" (Jer. 17:9)! Even with Christ, we can still be guilty of hating others and God. That's why John is writing to believers. He knows they are guilty of hatred and wants to address this matter so that they can move onto maturity. In order to mature, though, we need to face the reality that we really do hate, sometimes with feelings but sometimes with our behavior. Hatred needs to be repented of regardless of how we express or model it.

Now, let's take hatred and apply it to how we, as children, respond to our life experiences. I'll give you a four-step process:

1. By now, it's clear from what I've written that we are all born with desire—in particular, desire for relationship. We can't get rid of this desire. God has created it in us because we are created in *his* image. He is a relational God. Even the Trinity has relationship with each of its members. God the Father, God, the Son, and God the Holy Spirit all interact and relate to each other. Being created in his image means that, at our core, we long for relationship. We are created to have relationship with mommy and daddy first, followed by same-sex peers and then the opposite sex.

2. Because of sin's entering the world, humans sin against each other. Our fathers and mothers fail; our friends fail; all people fail. We are wounded. Now, a child has good resilience in relationship because he or she is created in the image of God. Eventually, though, continually being sinned against in the same manner over and over will lead to a child growing weary and breaking down. Proverbs 13:12 says, "Hope deferred makes the heart sick." We will do anything to overcome disappointment and continual discouragement. A child wants to avoid anything that continually causes pain. What happens if a child can't escape the pain being forced upon him or her? What happens if the child can't escape the abusive person? What happens when the emotionally absent father is never present for the child, who grows weary of feeling empty inside but can't find a way to get away from this pain? What happens if a child constantly longs for what he or she cannot experience with the mother and/or father? Answer: The child will shut down his or her heart. Dan Allender explained that the best way to shut one's heart down is to use the emotion of hatred. Since we can't get rid of desire, especially for longings for a loving mother and father, hatred is the strongest emotion that can push the desires away and cause us not to feel them anymore.

3. The problem is that we were created for relationship, so no matter what you do to get rid of that desire for relationship, it will not go away. The child may be successful at suppressing it, but the desire is merely masked and covered up. It's not gone.

4. As a result, the desire for relationship comes up another way. Think of a mountain stream flowing down the mountain and across meadows. Let's say an avalanche or mudslide takes place and blocks the flow of the stream. The stream doesn't stop flowing at its source just because there is blockage. The stream continues to flow and has to find another route to take. The same takes place with our desire for relationship. Putting up a block in our hearts doesn't stop desire for relationship, so it has to redirect itself in another way. This other path can reveal that it's a desire for relationship, whether we actually put a name to it or not. We may not be cognizant of this process at all, but our behavior tells the truth. Just as hatred is not necessarily felt, so our desire for relationship is not always necessarily felt. But our behavior often betrays us, showing what we really long for even when we deny it to ourselves.

I'll take this process and apply it to my life. As a child, I came into the world longing for emotional intimacy with my mother and father—to feel secure, known, accepted, valued, and loved. Once again, these desires are natural to me and cannot be removed. My relationship with my mother was a place where I felt a certain amount of security, value, and felt known and loved. My father was physically present, always providing financially for the family. We may not have had what others would consider the best clothes or other material items, but we never lacked in food, clothing, and shelter. So, in that regard, my father was awesome!

In addition, my father did not expose me to addictive behaviors like alcohol, drugs, or pornography. My family struggled in the area of food but this is a socially acceptable form of addiction. I wasn't exposed to being abused or called names. My father might have disciplined me inappropriately a few times, but most of the time he was appropriate in his discipline.

Where he lacked was in his ability to emotionally connect: to pursue me, to know me through conversation, to show me healthy physical affection. I remember my father apologizing twice to me, implying that he hurt me only twice, which is an inaccurate assessment of the relationship. I felt hurt by my father almost daily because he rarely ever spoke to me. As I shared earlier, my brothers had the same experience of our father.

During dinner one night, my father went to put food on my plate. As he lifted the plate, the edge hit my lip. He laughed and said, "Oops." I started to laugh and then burst into tears. My father got upset and left the table, calling me "sissy" as he left. What my father didn't know was that I was already feeling emotionally fragile because I had just had a fight with my older brother that was yet unresolved.

For children to have a parent relate to them in this manner leaves wounds. This kind of interaction isn't the worst thing that can happen between a father and son but the wound does still impact the heart of a son. Like the traumas we mentioned earlier, I didn't feel cherished and celebrated by my father. I didn't feel the experience of being a delight to him. Physical affection was so absent that I rarely remember moments of ever experiencing this feeling. My mother was the physically affectionate person in the home but even then this wasn't enough for what I needed. As we spoke about earlier, these absences leave traumas in our hearts.

As a result of feeling unseen and unknown by my father, a man who outwardly looks like a great dad, I started to close my heart to him. "If he doesn't want to be with me," I said to myself, "I don't want to be with him." When I reached adolescence, I actually hated my father in my heart. This feeling confused me because I couldn't point to any blatantly obvious behaviors that would indicate he is a horrible man or that I *should* hate him. I was a product of my culture, which only pays attention to severe and obvious behaviors. My feelings confused me only because I didn't understand what I really needed. Only as I became an adult could I come to understand what people need and what I specifically needed.

My hatred became strong not only for my father but for males in general. You may recall in a previous chapter when I spoke of how I was called "sissy" and "fag" regularly and experienced males as predominantly cold and unfeeling. My experiences with same-sex peers mimicked the distance and lack of intimacy I had with my father.

It's important to know that I did not see being a male as a positive experience, to the extent that I did not want to even consider myself a male. I was a bit turned off by the idea of being a male in this culture. What I was drawn to more was being androgynous—not being fully male but not fully female either. It's not that I felt like I was a female trapped in a male's body. I just didn't like the American version of being a male and felt the pressure to be this way, similar to my father. I didn't want to be like my father. I not only rejected him but also the concept of masculinity. I didn't like the idea of being masculine or being macho. There didn't seem to be any other models that reflected other options for masculinity.

However, my desire was to have a close relational connection with a man and to feel good about being male. Suppressing these desires resulted in my being drawn to males sexually. The mountain stream analogy I referred to earlier applies here. Suppressing desires does not make them go away, just as a mountain stream does not stop flowing simply because an avalanche happens and blocks it. The desires will bubble up another way. For males, the desires will bubble up in anger or sexual lust because these are less threatening emotions than disappointment and sorrow. For males with same-sex attraction, we have come to reject not only individual males but masculinity in general, typically because males have negatively impacted us. My father was the first male to impact me negatively, but he certainly wasn't the only one.

We need to be just as aware of how a child responds to what has impacted him or her as to what caused the impact in the first place. We can never look exclusively at the events, wounds, and traumas. Hatred of the same sex is a huge part of why someone has same-sex attraction. This has often not been valued as equally important as what happened to a child.

In the past, churches have often belittled the struggle of same-sex attraction by simply stating that it's a sinful behavior to avoid. Little has been acknowledged in terms of the underlying traumas and legitimate needs of an individual. Long before sexual activity manifests in a child or adolescent, sinful choices have already been made. Hatred is one of these sinful choices. Even though having hatred for someone who has harmed you is completely understandable, God still calls us to repent of the sin of hatred as we grow into adults.

Since the church typically does not understand this process within those who struggle, the response of the church has been just as harmful for men and women with same-sex attractions, thus tempting them more to battle this sin of hatred. In the next chapter, we will examine how the church has contributed to the struggle of hatred by sinning against those with same-sex attractions.

8

The Church: The Bad and the Ugly

A DIFFICULT CHOICE

"GOD HATES FAGS!" A demonstrator carried this sign while another yelled more hateful messages through a bullhorn. Leviticus 20:13, a verse often referred to by pro-gay advocates as a "clobber verse," was written underneath these words. The small group of demonstrators was led by Fred Phelps, the famous Baptist pastor of Westboro Baptist Church in Topeka, Kansas. (Fred Phelps passed away during the writing of this book.) Stunned by the harshness of their words, I slowly continued my walk toward the convention center.

Close to the doors of the convention center, a large rainbow of balloons caught my attention. Underneath the balloons stood a group of silent demonstrators called SoulForce, led by Mel White. Pastor White, who had been a ghostwriter for such spiritual leaders as Jerry Falwell and Billy Graham, had himself come out as gay years before. Taking an approach closer to that of Gandhi or Dr. Martin Luther King Jr., SoulForce demonstrates at various venues with silent protests, communicating their message of acceptance of homosexuality only with signs. Their approach was peaceful, inoffensive, and certainly more attractive to me than Fred Phelps' approach.

Was this the choice I had to make? Are these the only options for someone seeking to follow Christ?

I was attending an annual conference for a church denomination in Long Beach, California. I wasn't just attending but also testifying before committees about my transformation. I planned to encourage the denomination to remain faithful to God's ideals for sexuality.

As I entered the hall that morning, my heart was deeply grieved. I believed that God did not condemn those who truly sought him, but I also knew there was hope beyond acceptance. Were these the only two responses that the church had to offer? Was there not another option?

The presence of these two groups seemed to polarize the message: affirm homosexuality with humble and quiet reserve, or demonize gays and say they are going to hell. I prayed, asking God to reach both groups with his heart and desire. Thoughts stirred in my heart and mind as I prepared to testify.

A FAILURE OF THE CHURCH

After twenty years of ministering to those with unwanted same-sex attractions, I believe it's essential that I share with my brothers and sisters in Christ how I *perceive that* the church has failed. When Christians are confused about why some of those in the gay community hate Christians, there's obviously ignorance about what has really happened. In this chapter I will share only a few stories of what I have heard.

Approximately ten years ago, I began counseling a young African American male who had been involved in his church since he was a young boy. Seeking help, he confessed to his pastor his struggle with same-sex attractions. Not only was this young man attracted to males, but he was also constantly in turmoil due to his episodes of promiscuous sex with anonymous partners. One time, upon sharing with his pastor that he had failed yet again, the pastor responded, *"You might as well get castrated because that's the only way you're going to overcome your struggle."*

There may be many reasons for failure on the part of this pastor to adequately minister to the troubled young man as he sought counsel. Maybe the pastor felt no hope for his own struggles. Maybe he had nothing but simple answers to offer and jumped to a ridiculous option to hide his own inadequacies. How could his statement be an offer of the hope of Christ—or the hope of *anything*? I asked to meet with this young man and his pastor to offer support and try to engage in helpful dialogue, but the pastor refused. I never learned why he turned down this opportunity. Perhaps pride or suspicion about who I was got in the way, but the result was further rejection for this young man seeking help.

A man in his forties shared about a visit with his uncle, who happened to be a pastor. As they were talking, his uncle shared how a homosexual man came into his church asking for help. The uncle proudly told the man, "You want to go to the church down the street. We don't help your kind here." He arrogantly made this remark, not even realizing that the nephew sitting right in front of him had same-sex attractions. Do you think the nephew is going to feel encouraged to seek support from his uncle, or to experience compassion and love from his uncle?

While these examples of rejection in the church may seem extreme, I have repeatedly heard similar stories about what men and women experience in church. So I decided to conduct an anonymous survey to gain an idea of experiences men and women had relating to the church regarding same-sex attractions (SSA). The survey of over fifty people included men I had counseled, as well as leaders of ministries who had previously lived as a gay man or lesbian. Their comments include experiences of being ignored, suppressed, or rejected:

- I experience silence and apathy from my church.

- I had a gal confide in me about things that she was struggling with, including SSA. When she shared that, she said she didn't think I would understand. That was when I shared my testimony of how God took me out of homosexuality, and there is freedom and healing in Christ. Later, this young woman gossiped about my past with others in the church. After that, I became ostracized in that particular church by many.

- Some people in my church do not associate with me at all.

- Most of our members seem like they don't really care about it.

- I have watched people take a step back from me when you tell them your struggle. People love to hear the victory stories, but when that turns into actual current struggles—they freeze. People don't know how to love and keep loving when a person backslides and they need to walk through the valley with them.

A CHURCH OF SHEEP

As I began writing this chapter, I asked God for direction on what he would like me to address, and he led me to a passage in the book of Ezekiel. Here is a message that God spoke, thousands of years ago, to spiritual leaders with whom he was disgusted:

> Then this message came to me from the Lord: "Son of man, prophesy against the shepherds, the leaders of Israel. Give them this message from the Sovereign Lord: What sorrow awaits you shepherds who feed yourselves instead of your flocks. Shouldn't shepherds feed their sheep? You drink the milk, wear the wool, and butcher the best animals, but you let your flocks starve. You have not taken care of the weak. You have not tended the sick or bound up the injured. You have not gone looking for those who have wandered away and are lost. Instead, you have ruled them with harshness and cruelty. So my sheep have been scattered without a shepherd, and they are easy prey for any wild animal. They have wandered through all the mountains and all the hills, across the face of the earth, yet no one has gone to search for them.
>
> "Therefore, you shepherds, hear the word of the Lord: As surely as I live, says the Sovereign Lord, you abandoned my flock and left them to be attacked by every wild animal. And though you were my shepherds, you didn't search for my sheep when they were lost. You took care of yourselves and left the sheep to starve. Therefore, you shepherds, hear the word of the Lord. This is what the Sovereign Lord says: I now consider these shepherds my enemies, and I will hold them responsible for what has happened to my flock. I will take away their right to feed the flock, and I will stop them from feeding themselves. I will rescue my flock from their mouths; the sheep will no longer be their prey. (Ezek. 34:1–10)

Ezekiel is one of those long books in the Bible that seems to get read very little. Ezekiel was a prophet, and we often don't know what to do with the prophets who acted strangely and had dreams or visions. However, these were real people with real visions from God. I think they often freak us out because God really is speaking!

God was irked at spiritual leaders who were oppressive and neglectful of the very people God called them to shepherd, to care for and love. In their selfishness, they were harsh and cruel and left the sheep to roam on their own, vulnerable to being devoured. It took courage for Ezekiel to say this to God's people.

As I asked God what he wanted to say to me from this passage, the following thoughts rose in my mind:

> Many pastors have abandoned those they were called to love. They have chosen a religious perspective by choosing whom to love and how. They have forgotten that I have called them to love in my way, which calls them to care for the least of these, not the best. They choose comfort and acceptance from those they value—the corporate, the intelligent, the affluent—but they have forgotten that I came for the sick, not for those who don't need a Savior. Those in the gay community who once were in the church were my sons and daughters, and you left them to wrestle on their own, vulnerable to any belief or thought that would welcome them with open arms. And now they are lost without me. They are lost because of you, not because of their choices.

This is a bold statement, but I don't want to hold back. The church has forgotten our call to "love our neighbor" (Matt. 22:39) and "go and make disciples" (Matt. 28:19–20). If the church was faithful to this call, she would love those with same-sex attractions well, and would disciple them to be some of the spiritual leaders in the church today.

THE CHURCH IGNORES SIN

We're not going to address the argument in this chapter of whether you can be Christian and gay. What I'd rather state more boldly, and in a broader sense, is that I'm not sure how much those who profess to follow Christ, in general, really know Christ. We have Scriptures that state clearly that not everyone who professes to believe in Christ will be accepted by him (Matt. 7:21–23; Luke 13:22–27; James 2:14–25). In addition, Christ stated clearly that narrow is the path for those who are righteous and wide is the path to destruction (Matt. 7:13–14).

A liberal perspective on Scripture is not a new thing that resulted from Christians affirming homosexuality. There has been a neglect of the Word of God for many years.

How do I know this? For one, there is clear guidance in the Scriptures regarding God's heart for the poor. Let's take the sin of greed. Keeping most of our money for ourselves doesn't seem like a horrible thing to many of us Christians. However, when you look at the rest of the world, it doesn't make sense that we would keep so much for ourselves. "With less than 5 percent of world population, the U.S. uses one-third of the world's paper, a quarter of the world's oil, 23 percent of the coal, 27 percent of the aluminum, and 19 percent of the copper," reports Dave Tilford of the Sierra Club. "Our per capita use of energy, metals, minerals, forest products, fish, grains, meat, and even fresh water dwarfs that of people living in the developing world."[1]

Thousands of people die around the world each day because they don't have basics—not luxuries, but basics like food, clean water, medical care (such as aspirin), and clothing. Many of us have way more food than we need, waste more water than we'd like to confess, and have a closet full of clothes that would outfit most families around the world. When we live in excess and share little with the world, *thousands* of people *die!* This is not speculation but fact!

Our sin of greed causes thousands of people to die daily. Why belittle this sin and put homosexuality on a pedestal as being worse? If we really want to make a list of priorities in terms of sins, let's put greed as the number one sin. Plenty of this information is accessible to the American public, but we just choose not to be bothered with the needs of the world. Somehow, I don't think God affirms our excess while the poor pound on our doors for basic food and water.

Now, our sinning in other ways doesn't mean we should have a knee-jerk reaction and swing to giving license to other sinful behaviors like homosexuality. All sin matters to God and no one is worse than anyone else in the church. Some sins have greater earthly consequences, but sin keeps us from God no matter how little or small it is in our eyes. According to Romans 3, *all* have sinned and fall short of God's glory (v. 23), so all of humanity who is in need of a Savior, not just certain people. Throwing out homosexuality, along with all of the other sins, is not an option.

In judging homosexuality as a worse sin, some Christians like to quote Scripture verses that express how Sodom was destroyed because of the sin of homosexuality. But they often neglect one Scripture passage that gives a fuller picture, which also happens to be in Ezekiel. Listen, once again, to the words of Ezekiel: "As I live, says the Lord God, your sister Sodom and her daughters have not done as you and your daughters have done. Behold, this was the guilt of your sister Sodom: she and her daughters had pride, surfeit of food, and prosperous ease, but did not aid the poor and needy. They were

1. Scheer and Moss, "Use It and Lose It," lines 16–21.

haughty, and did abominable things before me; therefore I removed them, when I saw it" (Ezek. 16:48–50, RSV).

Sometimes pro-gay theologians will refer to this passage to state that Sodom's sin was *not* homosexuality. This is inaccurate as well. The "abominable things" included same-sex behavior and other sexual sins. Theologian Thomas Schmidt shares the following insight in his book *Straight & Narrow?*: "Various things were *abominable,* but since the word is used to describe sexual sin in the same chapter (vv. 22, 58), and since it refers to same-sex acts in Leviticus 18:22 and 20:13, the passage may imply quite the opposite of the revisionist claim."[2]

Revisionists argue that *abominations* refer to idolatry without implications for sexual sin. There was a larger sin problem with pride, gluttony, and the neglect of the poor, but sexual sin is not eliminated from the list of the sins of Sodom.

What we in the church have done is to create a list of which sins are worse than others. Even when we do this, however, we neglect other sins that are clearly ones that God hates. God hates pride and lying (Ezek. 16:48–50; Prov. 6:16–19, 12:22). He hates the neglect of the poor (Ezek. 16:48–50; Ps. 37:12–17; Jer. 5:26–29; James 5:1–6). Yet these sins are very present in the church today.

How often have you seen someone kicked out of church because they are prideful? How about being kicked out of church because that person neglected the poor? I personally have never seen such a thing in all my years of church attendance, membership, and leadership. Yet men and women with same-sex attractions have often been kicked out of the church because of their sin struggles. If we are going to kick people out of the church, let's at least be consistent instead of hypocritical (meaning we look at some Scriptures while neglecting others). If we did really follow through on this, our churches actually might be empty.

We as Christians are okay with sins like pride, gluttony, ignoring the poor, unforgiveness, gossip, and divorce. And then we wonder why some people have come to the conclusion that homosexuality is acceptable in God's eyes. God has made it clear in the Scriptures how he feels about the sins listed above. Why ignore what he says about these and then harp on the sin of homosexuality? Part of the reason some of the church accepts homosexuality now is because there has been rampant sin in the church, unaddressed, for many years.

2. Schmidt, *Straight & Narrow?*, 88. Italics in original text.

The church has a history of either ignoring homosexuality, calling people to suppress their desires without helping them, or rejecting them. I would add that we have failed in one other way: by affirming homosexuality. However, affirming homosexuality makes sense in a church culture that has a consistent pattern of not facing all her sins. We pick and choose what we want to address and demonize certain sins over others, thus demonizing certain people, or we dismiss a great many behaviors as no longer being sinful and give license to do as we wish.

REGARDING THE "GOD HATES FAGS" MINISTER

Before I discuss ways that the church has responded well, I would like to pause and comment about Fred Phelps, who was reported on in the media much more than any other Christian leader or group with regard to gays and lesbians. Fred Phelps was a pastor who led Westboro Baptist Church, an independent Baptist church based in Topeka, Kansas. Phelps's church is most known for demonstrating at various events, including military funerals, gay pride gatherings, and other gatherings and concerts with which they had no affiliation. The church's members saw it as their duty to warn others about God's anger. Westboro Baptist Church is the group I encountered and spoke about at the beginning of this chapter.

I would like to express my frustration with the bias and hatred of the American media, which reported Fred Phelps's activities over and over as if they represented the true church. Sometimes Phelps and his church were referred to as extremists, but the message was still that he was connected with those who call themselves Christians.

The media has been very careful to communicate that those involved in the 9/11 plots were *not* representative of Muslims in general. The Muslims involved in 9/11 were considered extremists as well, but no message was consistently communicated that they represent *all* Muslims. By covering Fred Phelps's group continuously, and not reporting on Christian groups opposing his message or doing the opposite of his followers, the media implied the insidious message that he and *all other Christians* are one and the same.

There are plenty of voices on the Internet with a plethora of opinions regarding homosexuality and the church. One I read recently is that of T.F. Charlton, who writes a blog about issues of gender and sexuality in Christian communities. On December 24, 2010, she wrote:

In its essence, what "mainstream" conservative Christians believe about LGBT people is no different from what Fred Phelps believes about them. I don't know . . . anyone from my old fundamentalist life who would walk around with a sign stating that a brutally murdered gay man is in hell, much less openly gloat about it. But apart from a very small handful of people, everyone I know from my former churches certainly believes that Matthew Shepard is in hell, along with anyone who died while living a "homosexual lifestyle." The fact that they don't walk around with signs declaring this doesn't make their beliefs any less hateful.

I grew up around these folks. Many of the Christians I knew were willing to state openly their beliefs that homosexuality should be a capital crime, that LGBT people are child molesters or rapists given the opportunity, or that AIDS was God's punishment for homosexuality. This wasn't so long ago . . . These beliefs have never been explicitly retracted or condemned in any of the communities I was part of.

A few isolated people—even some relatively prominent ones—have "repented" of being ignorant and fearful of LGB people, of being deceitful in their representation of them, and have even admitted to sinning in how they responded to the emergence of AIDS. And many prominent evangelical pastors today are downright skittish when it comes to the once ubiquitous rhetoric of "perversion" and divine punishment, favoring instead phrases like "sexual confusion" and "struggling with same-sex attraction," and talking about how homosexuals need "compassion" and "truth spoken in love" from Christians.[3]

In our culture, it is not unusual to throw out blanket statements as if they are fact. *If my experience matches yours, then it must be true for all.* But this is part of the immature relating as a culture that we spoke of in an earlier chapter. When we are immature, we throw out blanket statements and make generalizations, grouping people into categories rather than allowing for the complexity that exists among many people and many people groups. Perhaps Tope's experience truly was exactly as she stated. But does this represent all of Christianity?

How is this line of reasoning any different than that of someone who was molested by a homosexual man or lesbian? There are statistical facts to show that this type of molestation *does* occur. These aren't hidden facts.

3. Charlton, "Fred Phelps and Conservative Christians: Not So Different," lines 18–40.

However, it would be ludicrous to make the statement that *all* gays and lesbians are child molesters.

Some gay activists contend that Christians have elevated numbers of children being molested by homosexuals to prove that gays and lesbians are "worse" than heterosexuals. Let's not put any specific number on the horrible issue of child molestation. The fact that this occurs even once is concern enough for all of us! Even if it happens once to an individual, that individual might possibly conclude that *all* homosexuals sexually abuse children. Why that person who was abused comes to this conclusion may be understandable, but that person's perception is skewed by his or her experience. Maturity allows us to know that even if something happens, good or bad, we cannot make general, blanket statements. Complexity exists with all experiences, individuals, and groups.

To connect Fred Phelps with all Christians is a gross overstatement and neglects all the other Christians who haven't even had a chance to express their views on God, sexuality, or what they believe about men and women with same-sex attractions. I personally *cannot* say that Matthew Shepard is in hell, as Fred Phelps used to point out. How do I know? I'm not God. My understanding is that the only people who are going to hell are those who do not believe in Jesus Christ as the Son of God (Acts 2:37–39; Rom. 10:9–13). People don't go to hell because they are gay, and people don't go to heaven because they are straight! The *only* thing that saves us is faith in Jesus Christ—that's it!

Many Christians are certainly guilty in speaking incorrect theology with regard to salvation, sin, and following Christ. These false beliefs have influenced things that people say toward gays and lesbians. Often those who have studied the Scriptures well and seek to follow Christ as he called us are not heard or known by many in the gay community or by non-Christians in general.

Both the gay community and Christians are at fault for not truly knowing one another, seeking to be understood, and listening well to each other. If anything is going to improve between Christians and gays and lesbians, then we *all* need to repent of how we relate to each other.

I would also like to emphatically state that I believe Fred Phelps was *not* a Christian! In other books written by Christians, he has been spoken of in a gentler manner. I have no room for being gentle with individuals or groups who profess to be Christian but do not represent Christ or his church. Thomas Schmidt, once again, writes in *Straight and Narrow?*,

"Christians who cannot yet deal with the issues calmly and compassionately should keep their mouths shut, and they should certainly stay away from the front lines of ministry and public policy debate—not to mention television talk shows. Such people are hard to reach, because they suspect that those who call them to account are 'soft on sin.' They must be convinced that the way of Jesus is the way of the Wounded Healer, not the Holy Terror."[4] Preach it, brother Schmidt!

My testimony at the beginning of this book expresses how transformation of my sexual desires has taken place. Christ not only died on the cross and rose again to free me from the condemnation of my sin, but also to bring new life (Rom. 6:4; 2 Cor. 5:17; Eph. 4:22–24; Col. 3:10). My life has changed because I believe and follow Jesus. I am no longer condemned (Rom. 8:1), and I have taken on a new identity as a son of God. In Fred Phelps's words, those who are ex-gay, like myself, are *"filthy, lawless, irreversibly doomed beasts."* I am not any of these things! I am a son of God, loved by my Father in heaven!

Our understanding is that if we can't believe in the transforming power of Jesus Christ, then there is no hopeful gospel message. If there is no gospel message of forgiveness and transformation, then this is not Christianity but another form of religion. Call it something else but *do not* call it Christianity!

Perhaps I am arrogant to make such a bold statement. You can determine for yourselves whether I am incorrect in my theology or not. I am willing to be wrong but not willing to be silent on hateful behavior that is not reflective of any aspect of the Christian faith. And for those of you who like to put people in boxes, Fred Phelps was a Democrat! (Look up Fred Phelps on Wikipedia and you'll find his former political activities in the Democratic Party.) Let that confuse you for a while.

Our culture has had enough of seeing only the bad part of the church. I am a product of part of the church that did well. Several Christian brothers took the time to seek to know, accept, and love me well. If it wasn't for their love for me, I don't think I would be where I am today. Through their love and faithfulness to Christ, healing took place in my heart and I was freed from my same-sex attractions.

I don't want to end on a bad note but I want to communicate that how the church has responded in the past needs to discontinue. We need to

4. Schmidt, *Straight and Narrow?*, 172–173.

truly live like Christ calls us to. In the next chapter, I want to share the good stories of what God has done through the church.

9

The Church: The Good News

HOW THE CHURCH CAN GET IT RIGHT

OKAY, HAVE YOU HAD enough of my ranting and raving from the last chapter? I think I feel a bit satisfied getting all that off my chest. You have to understand that I have been carrying all this around for years without being able to express it fully.

But I don't think it would be helpful just to identify how the church has failed without also talking about how the church is starting to get it right. Across the country, the issue of homosexuality has gone through the roof of many churches. Some still choose to stick their heads in the sand, but many are exhausted from the confusion centering on the issue and are seeking guidance.

I want to state confidently that I believe homosexuality is not part of God's plan for our lives, in the same way that all of these other sins are not part of God's plan for our lives: pride, greed, divorce, unforgiveness, gossip, and sexual behavior of any kind outside of marriage. God wants a body of believers who are willing to give their lives fully to him, not rating sins but considering all of them important because of our love for him. He longs for followers who would give up *everything* for him and not put any of their natural desires above him (Matt. 22:37; Luke 14:25–33). This is impossible for us to do in our own power, but it is possible with Christ who encourages us through the body of believers (Mark 10:27).

My own story is an example of how God works and brings healing in the church. I had no confidence that my sexual desires could change. I believed that God did not desire sex outside of marriage in any way. The only other option to marriage is celibacy. I actually believed this and wanted to be faithful to him. So I thought I probably had to commit to a life of celibacy. This was a difficult decision at first but one for which I was willing to commit.

God had other plans. He brought a man named Rick into my life, who was the first man who loved me well. He loved me like a true father. He taught me about the Bible and prayer in ways that stirred excitement rather than boredom or apathy. Whenever he would go and share the gospel with other people, he would take me with him so I could watch, learn, and possibly be a part of the conversation. Hugs and expression of my value were part of my friendship with him as well. I longed for a man to pursue me, to not be afraid to express physical affection, and to communicate that I mattered. Rick did all of these things.

These desires I had were God-given desires that are in all of humanity. All humans desire to be known, to be accepted, to be loved. I just thought they were my own selfish desires because my observations of the church were that this was not a priority. The priorities were having church services, Bible studies, and programs. All of these things, however, didn't seem to focus on learning how to love people well, to meet the deep cravings of the heart that are present in all of us.

My contention is that if the church was living out the ways that we are truly called to love, then there would be less of a problem with all sexual sin because the deeper needs of our hearts would be met. Most people indulging in sex outside of marriage are not really looking for sex, even though they may think this very thing. What we are all looking for is intimacy, to be known deeply and loved anyway. Our pursuit of sex is an alternative because we can't seem to get our needs met in healthy, appropriate, God-given ways, so we settle for less and seek sex instead.

Sex is a false substitute for the real thing. We were never meant to have our deepest longings and needs met through the act of sex. Nothing in the Bible supports this perspective, even though the message of our culture consistently communicates that if you don't have sex in your life, you won't live. Excuse me for pointing this out, but I have never ever heard or read anywhere that someone died because they never had sex. In this regard, I don't see sex as a "need" that all of us must have met. We certainly desire it as human beings. The desire for it is natural to us and certainly a good desire, since God created it. However, his desire is that we would exercise self-control with regard to this desire, as with all desires.

Sex was meant to be for marriage, to seal the bond of the marriage relationship and be part of knitting spouses' hearts together more deeply. That's why it can hurt so terribly when you've had sex with someone and then you break up. The sex was meant to help bond you for life; then you rip your heart apart and expect to recover from this fairly well? We don't recover well from having lots of sex and then ripping our hearts apart from the ones with whom we were to spend the rest of our lives. That's not God's plan.

Rick modeled the true love of Christ in my life, and this fed my soul. My deeper needs started to be met. We were only close friends for a year before he had to move on, but that one year meant the world to me. I cried when he left because I greatly longed for what he had given me through his life.

God, however, continued to do in me what he had begun. Several other men were led into my life over the next decade. All of these men loved God, wanted to follow him with their entire lives, and wanted to obey him by loving people well. The way they lived paid off. Not only were my emotional needs met, but my sexual desires also began to change.

My desires didn't change because I focused on acting the right way sexually. Neither did they change because I just prayed about it. There is no such thing as "Pray the Gay Away," as some will mock. My desires changed because my true emotional needs were met deep within. These desires for love and affirmation from a father, from male peers, from those who should love me in the body of Christ are at the heart of same-sex attraction. When these needs are met appropriately and effectively, then I am filled and I no longer am compelled to meet my needs through sexual behavior. (There is much more to the complexity of same-sex attraction. I'm merely addressing one major aspect of the issue for myself. As mentioned before, there are sins to be repented of as well, such as the hatred discussed in chapter 7.)

Often many in the church will say they love, and this is true. But do we raise the bar to love at the level that Jesus modeled? He was willing to give up *all* his rights to become human and bridge the huge gap between God and humans. He brought healing and hope even to those who hated him. In fact, he willingly gave his life for those who hated him most: those who killed him. Verses like Philippians 2:5–8 state that we are to have the same attitude. The path for us is the *same* as that of Christ.

From the survey I conducted several years ago, here are some examples of those who experienced good things in the church:

- My husband and I, along with three others, did a five-week Sunday school class on responding redemptively to homosexuality. The twenty to thirty members who attended consistently encouraged us, prayed for us, and told us how helpful the class was.

- The counseling pastor who is directly over me has helped heal me of a lot of anger toward the church. I am no longer mad.

- After sharing about my same-sex attraction with my best friend, he hugged me and told me he loved me. He continued to be my friend and continued to be a safe place to work out my emotional codependent tendencies.

WHAT IT MEANS TO BE A TRUE BROTHER IN CHRIST

Years ago, I had the privilege of counseling Matthew (not his real name), who was married and had children. However, his attractions continued to remain strongly for men. No one in his life knew about his struggle, so when I brought up the idea of sharing his struggle with a friend, he responded, "I will never tell anyone about this struggle in my life."

I certainly understand the fear of not wanting to share about this with anyone. Opening up about my sexual attractions to my friends was not something that came quickly or easily. I feared losing their friendship as well, so I understood Matthew's reservations. However, I know how healing it can be to open up with trusted friends, and I also know how integral a part friends can play in walking alongside someone with this struggle.

I stated, "Let's just keep this on the prayer table for a while and ask what God desires."

Several months later, Matthew finally opened up to not only one friend but several. How Matthew's friends cared for him and loved him was amazing. He told me of one moment when, he embarrassingly confessed to one of his friends that it was difficult to be around him when he dressed scantily during the summertime. His friend, rather than responding with "Eww," said, "I'll do anything to help you out." This kind of response nurtured his heart in ways no counselor could nurture.

On another night, Matthew was in a small group with his friend, sitting directly across from him in a circle. Matthew's friend caught him looking at his crotch (not unusual for a man with same-sex attractions who may be tempted to look at another man's crotch, in the same way many men struggle looking at women's breasts). Matthew was horrified and embarrassed that he had been caught. His friend smiled, grabbed his infant son from his wife next to him, and placed his son on his lap. They both laughed and what initially was a shameful experience turned into another healing moment that did not part friends.

I am sharing what life can look like between friends when one struggles with same-sex attractions and the other does not. Friends who seek to understand one another can help each other, pray for each other, navigate through the confusing moments, and come out true brothers in Christ on the other side.

HOW TO SUPPORT A BROTHER OR SISTER IN CHRIST

Participants in my survey also expressed how Christian brothers and sisters could be of support to those with unwanted same-sex attractions in the church:

- Take time to understand the struggle. Read a book or two on homosexuality. Believe that God can and wants to bring healing and freedom to those with this issue, and that someone who has never struggled in this area can play a part in this healing

- Treat us as you would want to be treated, with grace and truth.

- Stand beside me . . . Understand that I did not choose this. My attractions are no more of a choice than theirs. Understand that, like them, I will sometimes make bad choices but that does not change my value to God or the body of Christ. Understand that part of the process is learning how to have healthy relationships . . . healing will not take place if I am not in community. You cannot expect me to get my life together and be all healed and then be ready to be a part of the body of Christ. I can only heal if I am a part of the body of Christ.

- The church needs to speak the truth in love. Some churches are harsh and condemning, while others love without challenging one to change. There needs to be balance and sensitivity to those who struggle. Most people only know about the stereotypes and they have no clue how same-sex attraction develops and what would help.

- Just treat them as people, share your lives, disciple in the day-to-day. They are aware and are offended when treated like a project. And also have patience. Though I never went back, my attractions didn't change until after nine years of intense struggle, and sometimes breakdown and breakthrough look a lot alike.

- Homosexuality is not airborne or contagious through casual contact. [A more humorous response, but certainly reflective of what some have experienced in the church.]

- Love them right where they are at—even if you don't understand. They need affirmation more than anything as a male or female, but they might not know how to receive it. The last thing they need is for others to try to fix them and give them "solutions." They just need to know they are loved. Be willing to stay with them in it for the long haul. Every person and situation is different. If you are expecting a cookie-cutter way to help, it won't happen. What might help one person might be completely different for the next. I think healing and helping others is to be evaluated on an individual basis and their situation.

- Be a safe place where there is no judgment. Listen first and ask lots of questions to hear adequately the intricacies of a person's struggle rather than just dole out condemnation for behavior and instill behavioral control. Be willing to go deep into a person's heart and let God meet you there to know how to love that person well.

Do any of these examples give you clarity on how you can begin to love those with same-sex attraction? Is it difficult, or do you think it's possible for you? How far are you willing to go to love like Christ called you?

Christ calls us to give up *all* for him. Don't settle for less. Don't settle for a church that wants comfort and safety along with following Christ. Comfort and safety are not on the pages of the New Testament. Complete denial of yourself and death are the call. If this is unappealing to you, then be honest and tell God what you feel. Ask him to give you the heart that you cannot create in yourself.

It's not like I'm exactly living out God's calling myself. I battle following my own selfish ways every day. My existence is a constant pursuit of giving up my life so that Christ can live through me. I fail and succeed all along the way. I am not discouraged because this is normal life. And when you follow a God who is ecstatic about his love for you, this path doesn't seem so horrible. It's difficult much of the time, but it's not a pursuit I regret.

10

Redemptive Suffering

A WOMAN CAME INTO my office, speaking of her struggle with same-sex attraction. At one point she uttered, *"God doesn't want me to suffer, does he?"*

I had some questions for this woman to help her consider an alternative way of thinking. But the first thing that came to my mind is what I have gone through in my own life. Life has turned out to be very different than what I imagined or fantasized about as a boy. As a boy, there was always hope for the future and a dream that could come true. Reality painted another story for me.

Just before entering adolescence, my family moved from a small town of 10,000 people to a city of over 150,000. Life is very different in a larger city. I discovered that being a new student in a new school, unknown to anyone, is a painful experience. Adolescent males, of course, relate at a very immature level, not seeking to know someone but, in their insecurities, compare their power and strength with other males.

The tougher males dominated my school. Being beat up and made fun of on a daily basis was my experience for almost three years in middle school. If I showed weakness in any way, I was seen as "gay" or a "fag." My own battle with shame prevented me from saying anything to my parents. I didn't feel seen or loved by my father, and I was afraid to tell my mother for fear of heaping worry upon her. Unknown to myself at the time, I lived under the false belief that I was responsible for how my mother felt and I sought to protect her from anything that might cause her worry.

How males treated me was a significant part of my story and impacted my struggle with same-sex attraction.

During this period of time, my family was attending church and had been ever since I could remember. This new experience of rejection and pain, though, really caused me to question my faith. Where was God? Would he not deliver me from these boys? Suffering has a way of bringing your faith to a clear bottom-line question: does God really love me and will he protect me?

Silence always communicates a negative message to someone who's immature and insecure. God's silence didn't win my heart but caused me to rage against him, demanding that he *care* about me and release me from this daily torment. During those three years, I spent almost every day eating lunch by myself. There were a couple of males who were willing to speak to me occasionally, acknowledging that I was a human being. My time with them, however, was minimal. Most of the time I was forced into close proximity to the males who hated and rejected me.

THE PREDICTABILITY OF CHURCH

Little did I know, this time in my life was not going to be the worst pain I would experience. But it started to change my perspective on life and challenge me in my faith in ways I had never been challenged before. Each day was scary to step into, and I constantly looked to the skies, asking God where he was and why he wouldn't deliver me. I did learn something in my faith: just because I desired something didn't mean I would get it—possibly ever. God never delivered me from the torment of those adolescent males and he didn't reveal himself to me in ways I desired at that time. So I was left with some conclusions:

1. Either God doesn't exist;

2. He's hateful and delights in seeing people suffer; or

3. Maybe life was different than how I saw things. Maybe God looked at and lived life very differently than I understood. Maybe life was different all around from what I had been taught.

One of my strengths is that I am incredibly loyal. I will remain faithful even to friends who are neglectful, or to a God who keeps silent. Sometimes I can be loyal to a fault, but when it comes to relationship with God, my loyalty has paid off. I have learned over time that conclusion number three was the answer to the questions I had about life. God looks at life very differently than I do, and I had to be willing to trust him while walking on this path of life, to be willing to see life and humanity through his eyes.

What causes me to bring the subject of suffering up with regard to same-sex attraction? The woman I referred to at the beginning of the chapter expressed a common belief among Christians I have counseled for the past twenty years. Often, men and women struggling with same-sex attraction have given up on their journey to overcome their struggles partly because of this false belief that seems to permeate American church culture. This false belief is that God does not want *me* to suffer. When I look at the American church, I can see where people are getting their perspective on suffering. The American church isn't necessarily a place where you can find help with serious struggle and pain. I'm not saying this for everyone. But those I have counseled for years have consistently given me the same message: "The church was not a place that helped me with my struggles."

Think about it. For those of you who have gone to church regularly, at any time in your life, church services are fairly predictable. You enter a church and are greeted and handed a bulletin that tells of the order of the service. You find a seat, progress through the service in a predictable way each week, and then exit and go home. Some of you find friends and family there and you socialize, sometimes going out to lunch. No one, though, spends time during the service bawling their eyes out all the way through. If someone does, few, if any, typically gather around to pray for that person or speak words of encouragement. Sermons are fairly safe, not really pressing on you in a way that leaves you feeling uncomfortable or convicted about your lack of love for others. Sermons are usually mapped out in a way such that you feel encouraged or like you've learned something. You walk away feeling good about having learned something, as if you had gone to a class on sociology at school.

MY STORY OF UNPREDICTABILITY

You may recall that I was pastor of a Sunday evening congregation made up of mostly homeless and poor people. Those of us who weren't homeless or poor were dysfunctional at best. Bringing a mix of people together who haven't learned how to relate well to each other or maybe don't associate with one another during the week, and you get a formula for lots of problems and conflict. I'll share a couple with you at this moment.

One week, the police came in and dragged someone out in the middle of service. That individual had gotten in a fight with a homeless person in the church service. Just before entering the church, the conflict led to one of them pulling out a gun.

I spoke with the officers about waiting until the service was over, and they said they had every right to interrupt. I appreciated their protection, but I felt a bit violated by their saying they could do whatever they wanted in my church.

The following Sunday, a young African American man was walking around the hallway scaring people, especially the young women. When I interacted with him, he acted strangely as well. I grabbed him by the shoulders and looked him in the eye and said he would either need to start talking to me or I would call the police. He expressed how he was having petit mal seizures because of his epilepsy, and this caused him to wander around acting strangely. He was feeling very raw and sensitive because he had just had a seizure. I asked forgiveness for my sternness, and we figured out how to help this young man that night.

That same day, a homeless person didn't make it to the bathroom in time, so one of the church members had to clean up a pile of poop.

My church probably doesn't sound very safe to many middle- and upper-class Christians. In fact, I told people that if they wanted to visit my church, they would probably feel very uncomfortable. The services were disrupted regularly by people who were drunk, angry, or snoring while sleeping.

Do homeless people belong in church? Should we keep them separate? I happen to believe that the homeless belong in my church service as much as anyone who is wealthy. However, bringing people together who have little in common and are not used to each other will not produce a comfortable or safe place. Would you be willing to trust Jesus to help you through church services that were unpredictable and unfamiliar? Would you see yourself as someone who could come and serve others, and not just go to be served?

My point is that even our church services convey the message that life is meant to be predictable and manageable most of the time. Only occasionally are there disruptions. My church, I have found, is a very rare experience in Christian culture. But this is not normal life, not for most people in the world. We lack the experience of seeing how Jesus Christ can enter the chaos of the world, of our lives, and bring beauty, hope, and salvation. We don't have to manage our lives so we can make everything work the way we want. We can actually enter life as it is and face the chaos and pain, without having all the answers, and see God provide in every way we need.

If you've never had this kind of experience, I want to ask you: Would you be willing to let go of your comfortable and predictable life to see how God wants you to live?

OUR NEED TO EXPECT SUFFERING

If we are going to call those with same-sex attraction not to act upon their desires, and invite them into struggle, then we as the church need to be willing to struggle ourselves first, to model for them what it's like to follow Christ in the midst of pain and difficulty. Those of us who have had same-sex attractions, or are in the middle of having them, *will* struggle with loneliness, confusion, uncertainty, anger, frustration, and heartbreak. Some have addictive behaviors that won't disappear immediately. Will those of you who have never had same-sex attractions lead the way in how to remain faithful to Christ while actually dealing with these emotions yourselves? Or are you too busy giving in to your desires and managing your life that you have little to offer those of us who do not sexually feel the same as you?

Most of us haven't heard from church pulpits about the experience of suffering and how this is part of our relationship with Christ. In fact, 2 Timothy 3:12 states clearly, "Yes, and everyone who wants to live a godly life in Christ Jesus will suffer persecution."

This begs the question, if we *aren't* suffering, then are we really living a godly life in Christ Jesus? I can't answer that question for you, but I do know that the Bible is not a stranger to the concept of suffering. If you read the Bible, you will see many people struggling and suffering, either because of the sins of others or because of their own sin. Sometimes suffering happens because it's just the result of sin being in the world and we are not always suffering for a "reason." A world full of sin is reason enough that each of us suffers.

There are numerous verses that speak to suffering being a normal part of a believer's life and warn us not to be surprised but to actually expect it (Rom. 8:17; 2 Cor. 1:5–7; 2 Tim. 1:8 and 2:3; 1 Pet. 4:12–13). Thinking that something is *wrong* when we suffer avoids certain aspects of reality. Maybe we are avoiding what we do not believe. Gerald May wrote a book on addiction called *Addiction and Grace*. Here's what he states about suffering:

> In our society, we have come to believe that discomfort always means something is wrong. We are conditioned to believe that feelings of distress, pain, deprivation, yearning, and longing mean something is wrong with the way we are living our lives. Conversely, we are convinced that a rightly lived life must give us serenity, completion, and fulfillment. Comfort means "right" and distress means "wrong." The influence of such convictions is stifling to the human spirit. Individually and collectively, we must somehow recover the truth. The truth is, we were never meant to be completely satisfied.[1]

Wow! How do you feel when you read that paragraph? Are you avoiding the reality that perhaps you were *never* meant to be completely satisfied on this earth?

I've asked that question of men in my support group for years, and the response is often anger or discouragement. Why? Because we've been sold a bill of goods; we've been lied to by those who should have taught us that life is full of suffering, not full of comfort and ease. In recent years, I've shared that I used to think that life would have occasional bumps and bruises, but that mostly things should go smoothly.

Now I know the truth. The truth is that life is mostly difficult and occasionally you have some nice moments. What I have learned more, though, is that God is present in suffering and that he reveals himself to me in ways that I never would experience if I kept working to rid myself of pain and suffering.

It's not that I think God *wants* people to suffer. We just can't help but suffer because we live in a world full of sin. I sin, you sin, others sin against us, and that impacts the world negatively with damage, sickness, and death. To try and escape suffering is to not face the reality of the way things really are. As believers, by not facing the way things are, we then end up limiting how amazing God is when he comes to us in our pain.

---

1. May, *Addiction and Grace*, 23.

I have learned what Dan Allender and Tremper Longman III shared in their book, *Cry of the Soul*: "Don't assume that resolving your turbulent emotions is the key to meeting God. It is actually within the inner mayhem of life that a stage is built for the intrusive story of his light and love. The absence of tumult, more than its presence, is an enemy of the soul. God meets you in your weakness, not in your strength. He comforts those who mourn, not those who live above desperation. He reveals himself more often in darkness than in the happy moments of life."[2]

I believe those who seek to affirm their same-sex attraction and project approval onto God are partly running away from the concept of suffering and pain. They are refusing to face reality as it really is: difficult, challenging, and painful on a regular basis. I believe they are trying to remove certain emotions and focus on what American culture constantly obsesses about: happiness. Their efforts are to control their world and eliminate pain as much as they can, and all the while they are missing out on experiencing God at a depth that can only be experienced in the midst of suffering.

I'm not saying that gays, lesbians, and transgendered people haven't suffered already. Many have suffered abuse in childhood, or from an insensitive culture that has rejected and hated them, or from Christians who have forgotten what it means to follow Christ and his commands. I'm just saying that to follow Christ *truly* will mean continued suffering, especially with regard to dying to sexual desires outside of God's will. Once again, Allender and Longman speak to this aspect of emotions:

> You are considered godly if you can handle difficult trials with a detached and apparently unruffled confidence. But this conclusion is wrong. There are times when lack of emotion is simply the byproduct of hardness and arrogance. The Scriptures reveal that this absence of feelings is often a refusal to face the sorrow of life and the hunger of heaven; it is not the mark of maturity, but rather the boast of evil (Isa. 47:8; Rev. 18:7). Our refusal to embrace our emotions is often an attempt to escape the agony of childbirth and buttress the illusion of a safe world. It is an attempt to deal with a God who does not relieve our pain. The presence of disruptive emotions that feel irrational or out of control is not necessarily a sign of disease, sin, or trauma. Instead, it may be the signal that the heart is struggling with God. Therefore, we must view the ups and

2. Allender and Longman, *Cry of the Soul*, 26–27.

downs of our emotional life not as a problem to be resolved, but as a cry to be heard.[3]

I know, right about now you are thinking, *"Thanks, Brad. I feel really great about life and God right now!"* To be sure, it's difficult to face the truth.

Many of you remember watching *The Matrix* movie trilogy. When Neo is faced with reality and Morpheus introduces him to the way things *really* are in the world, he freaks out. That can happen to those of us who have been duped into believing that life shouldn't be that hard or that God doesn't want me to suffer. I guess I am asking you to take the red pill, not the blue pill. Take the red pill and face the reality that many people in the world already know and believe: life is mostly difficult with occasional nice moments.

If you follow Christ, though, your suffering is not in vain. It's not a waste of time. Suffering will lead you in relationship with Jesus to depths you can never experience when life is going fine and you're managing and controlling everything. Letting go and trusting Jesus in the midst of continued pain is really quite an amazing experience.

In the next chapter, we will look at what can happen in our souls as we walk through suffering.

3. Ibid., 23–24.

11

How God Meets Us in Suffering

IF WE ARE GOING to have to suffer, allow me to give some reasons for suffering for us to cling to so that we aren't suffering without purpose. I'll share a few reasons and then explain what we can expect from Jesus in the midst of suffering.

1. GOD EXPOSES THE DARKNESS IN OUR HEARTS THROUGH SUFFERING.

Simone Weil said, "There are only two things that pierce the human heart: beauty and affliction."[1] God uses suffering because it's one of the few things that reaches our hearts. Have you ever noticed that most of the moments when you learned something significant were in the darkest moments of your life? This has been my experience. Perhaps this is why Ecclesiastes 7:3 states, "Sorrow is better than laughter because a sad face is good for the heart."

We don't look too seriously at our lives when things are regularly going well. But we are forced to look at what is present deep in our hearts when we are going through trials and tribulations. Isn't that what happened to Job? His distrust of God was revealed as he went through great loss, grieving and questioning God regarding the purpose of his suffering. Before his tremendous loss, I'm sure he wasn't thinking that he needed to grow in

1. Eldredge and Curtis, *The Sacred Romance,* 185.

his trust of God. The Bible says Job "was blameless—a man of complete integrity. He feared God and stayed away from evil" (Job 1:1).

However, as he went through suffering, his lack of trust in God as life hit him hard was exposed. In this instance in Job's life, we know the trage-dies were from Satan. But God allowed them in his life. Satan wouldn't have been able to strike Job so hard had God not allowed it. This is a disturbing example of how God allows suffering to take place in our lives, which leads me to conclude that he thinks completely differently about suffering than I do.

Perhaps suffering is *not* the worst thing that could happen to me. If suffering was the worst thing that could happen to me, wouldn't Jesus have died on the cross to save me from suffering? Perhaps the worst thing that could happen to me is explained by what Jesus went through. He suffered and died because my sins would only lead to my eternal death—complete separation from God for eternity. Separation from God is the worst thing that could happen to me, not suffering.

2. GOD WILL GLORIFY HIMSELF AND HIS CHARACTER THROUGH SUFFERING.

When I was attending classes at Moody Bible Institute, I had a theology professor who said, *"Remember, the most important thing in life is God, not human life."* I was offended by this remark. I bristled inside. My feelings, however, exposed what I truly believed. Deep down, I believed that my life mattered more than God and what he desires. Maybe some of you don't agree with this perspective, but I was forced to face this perspective and decide for myself: Is God more important than me or am I more important than God?

What I concluded would determine how I lived the rest of my life. I could look at life through the filter of me mattering more than God. In this instance, what I feel becomes more important than God, and what I strive after will focus more on my personal comfort and ease rather than on fol-lowing and serving him.

If God is more important than me, then my life can actually become dispensable for the sake of the gospel. Here are some Scriptures that sup-port the notion of God glorifying himself through suffering in our lives: 2 Thessalonians 1:4–6; 1 Peter 4:12–13; and 2 Corinthians 1:5–7.

3. GOD MAKES US MORE LIKE HIM THROUGH SUFFERING.

Throughout my life, I have found that I grow most during times of struggle. Often my perception of myself has been inaccurate, and difficulty exposed character issues that needed to be addressed. For example, when I worked at a Chinese restaurant and lived with Chinese roommates, I entered into this experience not thinking that I was prejudiced. However, as I worked, lived, and breathed with my Chinese coworkers and friends for two years, I began to notice a subtle belief surfacing: that I was better than them in how I lived and thought.

When I faced this reality, I was both surprised and disgusted with myself. I never thought I was someone who was prejudiced, but it was easy to believe this when my entire experience up to that point had involved living with only white, middle-class people. I was surrounded by white, middle-class people at home, at church, at school, and in my neighborhood. I learned during those years that living with people who are like me didn't challenge me in the least. When I started living with people who think and live very differently, I was challenged to decide which way was better, theirs or mine. The truth is that what I often called wrong was actually just different. But my issue of feeling superior caused me to call what was different "bad."

A true test of what's within your heart and mine is revealed when we are in close proximity and relationship to people with whom we have nothing in common. Jesus put it quite clearly, "If you love only those who love you, why should you get credit for that? Even sinners love those who love them! And if you do good only to those who do good to you, why should you get credit? Even sinners do that much! And if you lend money only to those who can repay you, why should you get credit? Even sinners will lend to other sinners for a full return" (Luke 6:32–34).

Basically, loving people who are like us is not a true test of character, nor is it even what love really is. True love, according to Jesus' standards, is loving how *he* defines it, which means loving people whom we might even call our enemies. That's a good example of going through trials and difficulties to expose what needs to be revealed so we can become like Christ and not just have an intellectual belief in him. He wants us to *be* like him, not just *believe* in him. Here are some Scriptures that support this perspective: 1 Thessalonians 1:6–7; Hebrews 5:8; James 1:2–4; and 2 Corinthians 12:7–10.

4. WHEN YOU CHOOSE TO SUFFER, YOU HAVE CHOSEN TO NOT SIN.

What I mean by this seemingly unbelievable statement is that if I choose to let myself suffer, rather than meet a need on my own apart from God, I'm most likely not going to make a sinful choice. Often, suffering is what I experience when I choose not to sin, because I allow myself to feel the uncomfortable feelings I am trying to escape when I make sinful choices.

I have learned that we are typically striving to meet a need when we sin. Sinful behavior is usually intertwined with legitimate need. So, for example, if I am having sex with someone outside of marriage, the legitimate need is that I long to be loved and accepted. However, if I can't get this need met in the manner or timeframe that I desire, I might take matters into my own hands and meet this need through sex, whether it's with someone of the opposite sex or same sex. Either way, we are stepping outside of God's desire for us, and meeting needs out of our own sinful choices.

If we're *not* going to make a sinful choice to try and meet our needs, I think we often think that we will feel good about our choices. The truth is, though, choosing not to sin doesn't always make us feel good. Often we are still left feeling the weight of that legitimate need: that need for healthy physical affection, that desire to be seen and loved, and the like. The uncomfortable feelings remain.

I actually think this is one of the reasons we get mad at God. We don't like following his path and then not necessarily getting our needs met. We are challenged at this point in our belief systems. Does God take priority over my needs or do my needs take priority over him? I can't make that decision for you, and you cannot make it for me.

Now, this question does not mean that God will *never* meet your needs, but neither is it true that meeting our needs is something that God is *required* to do. There is nothing in the Bible that says that God *must* meet our needs. However, he chooses to because he is a God of love who cares for his children.

When our needs are not met in the timeframe we desire, we might experience pain and suffering. The reasons I've just given you for suffering are what you can turn to then to help you keep going and not give up on God while you struggle.

There is more going on in our lives than getting our needs met. God wants us to become like Jesus. In order for this to happen, he must reveal our brokenness so we can be free from our sin and live as he called us to live. Peter states clearly this concept that if we don't sin, we are often making the choice that involves suffering instead: "Since therefore Christ suffered in the flesh, arm yourselves with the same way of thinking, for whoever has suffered in the flesh has ceased from sin, so as to live for the rest of the time in the flesh no longer for human passions but for the will of God" (1 Pet. 4:1–2, ESV).

We don't have someone who cannot sympathize with our struggles. Jesus Christ knows about the challenge of choosing between what he desires and God's will. We see this in the Garden of Gethsemane when Jesus is praying (Matt. 26:36–43). Jesus' soul was crushed to the point of grief. His decision was difficult. He understood the choice between doing what he desired and choosing to follow God instead. If Jesus chose not to suffer on the cross, he would have been choosing sin instead of God's will. Since he chose to obey God, he suffered and died. We are told in 1 Peter 4 to have that same way of thinking, to be willing to set our desires aside for the sake of God's will being done.

Suffering is not an option; it is mostly likely a requirement. We, however, don't have to face these challenging choices without Jesus understanding and supporting us. Look at these verses and what they promise us in the midst of suffering: 2 Corinthians 1:3–7; 2 Thessalonians 1:5–6; Hebrews 2:18; Hebrews 13:5; 1 Peter 3:14; 1 Peter 4:12–13; and 1 Peter 5:8–10.

THE CALL TO DO WHAT JESUS DID

Some of you may read this list and, in the midst of your pain, you may still think to yourself, "Yeah, but this doesn't feel like enough. I still feel lousy." Remember that Gerald May said we will never be fully satisfied. I think you and I need to ask ourselves what more God needs to do if we are not satisfied with what Scriptures say. I mean, what are we expecting? The world to bow down and worship us? Honestly, sometimes I think that's *exactly* what I want! But I need to make a choice as to what I am going to do: let go of what I want and cling to God's desires, or give in and just worship myself by indulging in whatever I want.

Here's one last quote from Gerald May: "To love as a child of God is to live with love and hope and growth, but it is also to live with longing, with aching for a fullness of love that is never quite within our grasp. As attachments lighten and idols fall, we will enjoy increasing freedom. But at the same time our hearts will feel an even greater, purer, deeper ache. This particular pain is one that never leaves us."[2]

Remember: our goal on earth should never be complete freedom from pain. Our goal is to obey Christ and experience what he has to offer us in the midst of our pain and painful choices. Some of you feel too much pain because you haven't had your wounds completely mended yet. There is still damage in your heart that needs attention. Unforgiveness may dominate your heart. You can never be free from the pain that this brings unless you actually forgive people. It's difficult to do, but forgiving releases you from a certain amount of pain in your heart.

Some of you still feel the pain of loneliness and rejection. God is very aware of your pain and he knows exactly which pain comes from your sin, which comes from Satan, and which come from the sins of the world.

As you heal from your wounds, as you grow in your ability to resist Satan's attacks, as you grow in your security and the pains of this world don't completely overtake you, don't be surprised if there is still an ache in your heart. It's diminished but it may not be completely gone. As Gerald May states, it is purer, so it will feel different. You and I want to move toward pure pain, not pain stained by wounds and sin. This pain feels different. It's something you become used to living with and not seeing as an enemy.

For those with same-sex attractions, make the choice to say no to acting on your desires. Seek to put Jesus Christ before you and what you desire. Let him take your desires and shape them into his desires.

For those of you in the church who've never had these types of attractions, will you model for your brothers and sisters what it's like to suffer in obedience to Christ? Will you make choices not to divorce and to stay in difficult marriages? (Not abusive marriages, mind you, but difficult ones.) Are you willing to give up some of your personal material comforts so others in the world can have food, water, and medical attention? Will you seek to forgive people who have harmed you rather than leaving a line of damaged relationships behind you? Will you model staying in relationship with people you have nothing in common with, so you can learn what it *really* means to love?

Unless the church is willing to step into suffering for Christ in every way, we will have little to offer those in the gay community who want to follow Christ and die to their sexual desires. Let's walk *together* with our Christian brothers and sisters, those with same-sex attraction, and model

2. May, *Addiction and Grace*, 179–80.

together what it means to live a life of dying to self, that Christ might live fully in us.

12

Be Not Afraid—Listening to an Angry Culture

THE NIGHT WAS COLD. There were few patrons in a bar that I was trying for the first time. My street partner, Vincent, and I moseyed up to the bar and ordered a couple of Cokes. Vincent started talking with someone, and I sat quietly at the bar. As I was praying, a man came over to me and started asking about my button. After I expressed our motto phrase of talking to anyone about God who was interested, he hurled a few insults at me and stated, "I know what you're like! You're homophobic, bigoted, and a hateful person!"

I had never met this man before and was actually feeling rather tired that night. I wasn't feeling very patient for a difficult conversation.

As the man continued his tirade, and as I became weary of his insults, I yelled back, "Well, do you know what I think of you?"

He retorted, "What?"

"I think you are a decent person and we can have a decent conversation!"

My response threw him off. He stopped and really didn't know what to say.

In the pause, I asked what caused him to be so angry toward Christians. Surprisingly, without ranting in return, he was able to express the painful treatment he'd experienced in his life from those who professed to follow Jesus.

At that moment, I asked him for forgiveness for how he had been treated.

We continued our conversation for another hour and had a great talk about what was important and relevant about Jesus Christ.

At the end of our conversation, he said, "You know, you're a really nice guy."

I responded, "You are too."

How did we go from yelling at each other to ending a conversation complimenting each other? My guess is that most of you would be completely frightened by someone beginning a conversation yelling at you, and most of you would probably leave the place. However, learning how to not be controlled by others' emotions and staying present in a conversation can reap great benefits, including eventually sharing the hope that we have, not regarding sexual orientation and attraction, but in our relationship with Jesus Christ (1 Pet. 3:15).

MOVING FROM FEAR TO CONVERSATIONS

I have observed, in normal interactions and during speaking engagements in various venues around the country for the past twenty years, that a large percentage of Christians who believe homosexual behavior is wrong feel threatened and scared, and avoid sharing their opinion in a public setting that's not Christian. Certainly one of the reasons for this silence is the fear of being labeled and associated with vocal people like Fred Phelps, who have done a lot of damage in how people perceive the Christian community. Those who are more vocal tend not to reflect the true values of the kingdom of God, including humility and compassion. Thus some in the gay community believe that Christians, as a whole, are hateful people.

At one time, conversations in which different perspectives were expressed were a normal part of learning on college and university campuses. However, there has been a change in philosophy, especially toward issues like same-sex attraction, such that differing beliefs cannot be expressed. In fact, anyone who does not endorse living as a gay man or lesbian is automatically labeled as homophobic or bigoted.

I recently had lunch with a friend who is taking classes at a Christian college. When asked what the psychology professors' perspectives were regarding same-sex attractions, he expressed that he could "tell" which professors hold a traditional, Christian view on homosexuality and which have a more accepting perspective, even though he has rarely heard anyone express an opinion clearly and publicly, if at all. This was at a *Christian* college setting, where traditional Christian beliefs, along with other perspectives, should be allowed to be shared! Shouldn't an expression of ideas be encouraged, even regarding important personal matters? What causes us to be defensive and reactive?

My personal belief is that effective communication has to be taught. Even when we have been taught, we need to practice talking with people about cultural issues, spiritual beliefs, and personal feelings. When my sons were five-year-olds, I certainly didn't expect them to know how to talk about something like politics or comprehend Democratic or Republican values. They were too immature to understand relational complexity. Building relational skills and learning how to talk about easy and difficult matters takes lots of years of practice and time.

I fear, though, that most people do not learn these skills in the home. Many people come from homes where the parents or adults modeled insecurities and inferiority complexes and reacted emotionally to people whom they felt threatened by. Differing perspectives were seen not as something worth considering but as beliefs that needed to be immediately rejected. Most of us have seen adults sometimes sacrifice everything just to be right. Perhaps we have also done this.

Efforts to not be wrong dominate conversations about the gay community, as do prejudices from both the Christian community *and* the gay community. Some Christians view gay people and think they *know* what kind of people they are. They see them as definitely less moral. They could never imagine a gay person being *more* moral than them or believing in Jesus Christ. Some people in the gay community are equally guilty, thinking they know exactly what Christians think and how they are going to treat gay people. They think, "Christians are bigoted, homophobic, backward thinking. They couldn't possibly understand what it's like to be gay." Sometimes we come to these prejudices because we have actually had a bad experience with a particular person. But just because we have bad experiences with someone who is gay or someone who is Christian does not mean we have the right to place all gay people or all Christians in the same behavior pattern. We can't think, "They are all hateful people."

MOVING AWAY FROM BROAD BRUSHSTROKE THINKING

I remember having a conversation with a friend, who is a pastor, and another friend, who is gay. At one point, my gay friend proclaimed, pointing at my pastor friend, "I really have a beef with your church. I don't know how you can claim to be a Christian and yet be against homosexuals and those who get an abortion, and support the war."

I interjected, "Wait a minute. Let me ask you a question. Do all gay people think exactly the same way about every controversial issue?"

He responded, "Of course not. That's ridiculous."

I stated, "Well then what makes you think that all Christians think the same way about these same issues? In our church there are people who are against abortion and those who support it. There are Democrats and Republicans. There are those who believe homosexual behavior is wrong and those that believe God is okay with people being gay. There are people for the war and people against the war."

After pausing a moment, he stated, "You're right. I'm sorry."

You see, he was gravitating toward what is familiar and common behavior in the United States. We don't relate to each other as unique individuals. Then we come up with broad brush strokes about how this group of people is and what that group of people believes, not really knowing if it's true or not. We are unable to single out a person as unique and see that that person might think differently than the rest of the individuals like them. A similar type of immaturity occurs when a white person says they know how African Americans feel because they have a black friend. You mean all black people think the same way about everything? That would be ludicrous thinking, but that kind of relating often goes unchallenged in discussions about the issue of same-sex attractions, similar to how it has been unchallenged in conversations about race, religion, and politics.

We as Americans often avoid the more complex way of communicating with people, which is to seek to know each person uniquely. There will certainly be commonalities that exist among groups of people we identify as gay, Christian, Muslim, African American, etc. But we would be dishonoring people if we thought we knew everything about a group of people just because we knew one person among that group.

SECURITY: THE CORNERSTONE FOR BETTER RELATING

What causes us to relate in this manner? My belief is that we go to great lengths to prove we're right because our security is not established in the right place. Young adults and older adults who model impatience in public discourse regarding homosexuality—or any other controversial issue, for that matter—are merely individuals who have not found security in the right place: the fact that we have value merely because we are created by God, and Jesus Christ did everything to prove we matter by dying on the cross for us.

Christians and non-Christians alike miss out on the basic, fundamental belief that being created in the image of God automatically gives us value. As C. S. Lewis said, "There are no ordinary people. You have never talked to a mere mortal."[1] We are much more than mere mortals. We are men and women created by God, valuable enough that God would send Jesus to die for us, even while we were his enemies (Rom. 5:10; Eph. 2:3–7). If our foundation of security and value is not in the right place, we will grasp at anything to find value and affirmation, and we will fight to never be wrong. We will find our identity in the wrong places and defend that identity, whether it's true or false.

So the first step for us as believers is to make sure our own identity is secure in the right place. You are a daughter of God; you are a son of God. You have infinite value simply because you are created by God. You are loved deeply by him and accepted. He knows you completely—all your strengths and personality traits. He created you that way. He also knows your weaknesses, your failures, your dark secrets and sins. Yet this does not turn him away because Christ's death and resurrection removes any condemnation, any reason for God to reject you (Rom. 8:1, 31–39). You are fully known by him, fully accepted and fully loved.

Rest in this truth, Christian brothers and sisters! It's time you truly believed it not just in your head, but in your heart as well. Only as you walk in this confidence and peace are you able to enter a world that's hostile and not be afraid or intimidated by those who will reject.

FACING THE HOSTILE

Several years ago I was asked to come and do a presentation on my perspective on homosexuality at the University of Chicago. The ministry Cru was sponsoring the event, and there were over a hundred people present. Most of those listening were individuals who identified themselves as gay *and* Christian. I presented for half an hour and then opened up the rest of the time for questions. During the Q&A, most of the people present proceeded to lambast me and discredit everything I had said.

1. Kinnaman and Lyons, *unChristian*, 205.

One of the main points I made was that all of us are broken. I made this statement based on Romans 3, where Paul says,

> No one is righteous— not even one. No one is truly wise; no one is seeking God. All have turned away; all have become useless. No one does good, not a single one. Their talk is foul, like the stench from an open grave. Their tongues are filled with lies. Snake venom drips from their lips. Their mouths are full of cursing and bitterness. They rush to commit murder. Destruction and misery always follow them. They don't know where to find peace. They have no fear of God at all. (vv. 10–18)

My thought was that if I used a "safer" word, people might be willing to hear the rest of what I was sharing. From my perspective, I was putting us all on the same plane, the same level in terms of our common condition.

However, the response I got was not what I expected. The majority of the audience was *offended* that I was saying we are *all* broken. These are people who *profess* to be Christians! Do they understand the basic premise that all have sinned and fall short of the glory of God (Rom. 3:23)? Their response revealed to me that they have yet to fully accept the full message of the gospel. If you can't get to the place of admitting your need—that you are a total mess in need of a Savior—then you will not understand the death and resurrection of Jesus Christ.

Since I understood the basic gospel message, and since I *knew* who I was, I was unmoved as the insults and mockery continued. I was able to respond calmly and to the best of my knowledge. I never claimed to know everything, so when I didn't know the answer to a question that was asked, I simply responded that I didn't know. My goal was to share what I believed, in hopes that they would listen and understand and perhaps shared what they believed—but in a respectful and humble manner. What I got was arrogance and childishness!

One friend who came to listen to the exchange later told me, "Wow, you seemed really relaxed." I truly was, but that only happens when I have a firm conviction inside that I have value and am loved by God. It's all right for people to hate me because their approval is not what I seek. I don't need their approval. However, I am responsible for being loving and respectful, even in response to those who express hatred for me (Luke 6:27–36).

Prideful and hateful responses were a reflection of the lack of security present in their own hearts. People are not defensive and don't attack when they are secure. If I had attacked back, even in my heart, I would have been verifying that my security wasn't established yet by being sinful in my response. Remember that my behavior tells the truth. What I say does not, unless my actions and words match.

I've been on panel discussions at Purdue University in West Lafayette, Indiana; Indiana University-Purdue University Indianapolis in Indianapolis, Indiana; as well as Crossroads Bible Church in Indianapolis. In two of those settings, where the discussion took place in a secular setting, opponents of my perspective sought to insult and mock me when I shared what I believed. When I was in a "Christian" setting (a church building), opponents were careful and seemed to be more respectful. However, the same people present in the secular settings were present in the church setting. Their behavior was not consistent but changed with the circumstances. Someone who is secure maintains the same behavior in all settings and models consistency.

In order for us to interact as healthy followers of Jesus, we need to change how we have conversations about homosexuality. In the next chapter, I will introduce some dos and don'ts to help you with future interactions.

13

Elevating the Conversation

OPERATING OUT OF THE perspective that we are all broken people in need of a Savior, and that we as Christians *can* model maturity in our conversations by not being reactive to people's emotions, what steps can we take to relate differently with those who disagree with us on the matter of same-sex attractions? How can we keep the dialogue open with those in the gay community or those who profess to be Christian and identify as gay?

Following are some dos and don'ts to keep in mind as you seek to relate to and love people as Jesus called us to. Regardless of your past experiences with people and where you are now in your journey, always remember that Jesus calls every follower of his to make disciples, to reach out and love anyone in the world. Peter clearly says in 2 Peter 1:3–7 that, for the Christian, our ultimate goal is to have love for *everyone*. Even though it's an overwhelming task to think that we could possibly love everyone, I know this is my line in the sand. When I've crossed over this line, I know I'm finished growing as a believer. Of course, I'm not sure any of us will reach this, but who knows what can happen when we fully trust God with our lives? So here are don'ts for when you are talking to a friend or someone whom you just met:

DON'TS

1. Don't make same-sex attraction the main focus.

The main issue is always Jesus Christ. So your first task is to find out if this person has any faith in Jesus. If not, then that's the focus. It's not pointing out what's wrong with homosexuality but what is wrong with all of us as humans—our desperate condition and need for a Savior. Remember that we can't assume that people understand the concept of sin, so this has to be explained. Also remember that our most offensive message is not that homosexuality is a sin, but that Jesus Christ is the only way to God.

Recently I had a conversation with a gay friend of mine. He knows my position on same-sex attractions and stated that the Scriptures referring to homosexuality were misinterpreted. Rather than address this point, I asked him if he thought it was okay for people to have a sexual ethic. I explained that what I meant was that we have laws against certain sexual behaviors: rape and child molestation. People will be legally prosecuted if they participate in this kind of sexual behavior. These laws reflect a sexual ethic and show that we believe this sexual behavior is wrong. He agreed and believed it was a good thing for people to have their own personal sexual ethic.

I followed up with another question. What if Christians believed that having sex with someone of the same gender was wrong, whether you agreed or not with how they interpreted the Bible? Was it wrong for them to have this as part of their sexual ethic?

He said that he actually wasn't opposed to Christians having this as part of their sexual ethic. He was opposed to how they communicated this: in a judgmental and hateful manner. I was intrigued that he wasn't offended by Christians taking this perspective. He quickly followed up, asking me if I believed that Jesus Christ was the only way to have a relationship with God. This position was more of an offense to him than to say homosexuality was wrong. He could be patient with a Christian who says homosexuality is wrong if they aren't bullying and judgmental in their approach. However, to say that there is only one God and that Jesus is the only way to God comes across as much more restrictive and exclusive.

If you are not prepared to talk about your position on Jesus, then you need to make sure you understand and have full belief in this yourself before you start talking about any other controversial issue like homosexuality. Same-sex attraction is not our most difficult conversation; Jesus will always be our most difficult conversation to an unbeliever.

If someone claims to be a Christian, then your approach is still going back to Jesus. The questions change, though:

a. Does Jesus give guidelines on sexuality? What commands related to sexuality does he affirm?

b. Are you willing to give your life to him fully, even if that means not acting on the sexual desires you have? In following Christ, would you sacrifice acting on your sexual desires?

c. How can we study and discuss this together? What steps can we take to learn about Jesus' perspective?

The goal is always to strive to keep the conversation open and truly study and learn. This may mean that you are willing to read a pro-gay perspective. I've read several pro-gay books written by seminary professors or pastors who are gay or affirm homosexuality. It's imperative that I understand their position so I know how to relate in an informed and loving manner. The more I understand the opposite opinion, the more I have found even stronger support for my position.

2. Don't try to fit in!

Realize that your perspective could be a less and less popular position in culture and sometimes even in parts of the church. Listen to what Brené Brown says about the concept of "fitting in": "One of the biggest surprises in this research was learning that fitting in and belonging are not the same thing. In fact, fitting in is one of the greatest barriers to belonging. Fitting in is about assessing a situation and becoming who you need to be in order to be accepted. Belonging, on the other hand, doesn't require us to change who we are; it requires us to be who we are."[1]

Be who you are, not who you think other people want you to be so you can be accepted. Do you know who you are in Christ? Are you secure in being a son or daughter as the foundation for your identity? If you don't have Christ as the foundation, then you will most likely flex and change your positions in various situations. People know when you are trying to fit in, actually, and they typically don't respect it even though it seems like you want to agree with them.

---

1. Brown, *Daring Greatly*, 232.

There's no need to apologize for who you are and what you believe. As a human being, you are created by God and have great value. Remember, most people are not okay with what is *different*. Those with whom you speak may not be able to respect *your* differentness, but you can model it for them and show that you can hear and understand their position.

3. Don't let your emotions be influenced by how others feel.

Then you are forgetting who you are. Just because others are angry or frustrated doesn't mean that you are the one responsible for them feeling this way. Remember, a disproportionate reaction is always about the other person's issues. Now, this doesn't give me license to be a jerk and be insulting and not compassionate myself. I'm always called to be humble and compassionate.

Brennan Manning understands what it's like to fail and feel the pressure from others to be something he's not. He addresses the importance of living freely in Christ rather than living in bondage to people and how they treat you. Read this remark from his book, *The Ragamuffin Gospel*: "Freedom in Christ produces a healthy independence from peer pressure, people-pleasing, and the bondage of human respect. The tyranny of public opinion can manipulate our lives. The expectations of others can exert a subtle but controlling pressure on our behavior."[2]

Who knows why people get angry? You can't assume that their anger toward you is really why they are upset. Let them vent. Let them give voice to their feelings. You may be the first person who genuinely listens to them when all others don't hear or don't validate what they are feeling.

This leads me to my list of dos.

DOS

1. Do ask good questions and listen.

I love this quote by Max Ehrman, who was an American writer, poet, and attorney from Terre Haute, Indiana. This is his perspective on listening: "Speak your truth quietly and clearly; and listen to others, even to the dull and the ignorant; they too have their story."[3]

2. Manning, *The Ragamuffin Gospel*, 146.

3. Cavinder, "Desiderata," 14–15; Platt, *Respectfully Quoted*, 212.

Now, you could interpret his comment as actually calling some people "dull" and "ignorant." Those in the gay community are *not* dull and ignorant, but even if you were low enough to have this attitude, he's making a point. You can look down on someone but that person has a story, a story worth knowing. When you tell your truth, remember that speaking quietly and clearly will always come across much better than yelling at someone. This is consistent with what Peter says in 1 Peter 3: "And if someone asks about your Christian hope, always be ready to explain it. But do this in a gentle and respectful way. Keep your conscience clear. Then if people speak against you, they will be ashamed when they see what a good life you live because you belong to Christ. Remember, it is better to suffer for doing good, if that is what God wants, than to suffer for doing wrong" (vv. 15–17).

Remember, most people in our culture don't listen well. We are mostly interested in saying what we think and feel rather than listening first. Love other people like Jesus called us to, listen first, and then speak gently and humbly.

2. Do share about your own story.

What better way to talk about Jesus than to share your journey in seeing your own broken condition and seeing Jesus as the answer. Be clear about what sins convicted you to see that you were a bigger mess than you realized. Prove that homosexuality isn't the worse sin by sharing your conviction about your own sin that's different but no less important.

Jesus healed a man from blindness in John 9:24–25. The man being healed was confusing and troubling to the Pharisees, who wanted to understand this situation. The man didn't know how to explain what happened to him, but this is how he responded to the Pharisees at one point: "So for the second time they called in the man who had been blind and told him, 'God should get the glory for this, because we know this man Jesus is a sinner.' 'I don't know whether he is a sinner,' the man replied. 'But I know this: I was blind, and now I can see!'"

This man didn't know the answers to all their questions. All he knew was that once he was blind and now he could see. Once he was one way, and then Jesus' coming into his life made a complete difference.

That's my story. I may not know everything about the questions pro-gay people have for me, but one thing I can state without a doubt: once I *only* had same-sex attractions, and now I haven't for twenty years.

You have the same story of how your life changed when Jesus came.

3. Do talk about the issue of same-sex attraction.

There's no need to be ashamed of your position, but speak with an attitude of love. Keep in mind, though, that just because someone else wants to make gay identity the main focus, that doesn't mean you have to make it the main focus. Remember that our main understanding is first: knowing who we are in our identity as men and women created by God. Once we have relationship with him we become sons and daughters.

Out of this identity come our behavior and the motivation for our behavior—because we *love* our Abba Father, Daddy, not because we have to obey him. This means everyone makes sacrifices to be like our Father because all of us have a nature that is exactly opposite of the kingdom of God. So all of us sacrifice sexual desires, as well as other desires, to be in line with Jesus' plan for us in following him and becoming like him.

When I first began doing street outreach in Chicago, for the first six months I felt a dissonance in my heart. I was telling people that God loved them but I wasn't necessarily always feeling this love from him. I had already worked on much of my relationship with God, addressing feelings of anger and abandonment I felt from him. But there was still something in my heart that didn't feel right.

So I began praying about this, asking God to have me *feel* his love because I didn't want to tell others that God loved them and not feel it for myself. I can't remember the exact number of months that went by, but I can tell you that after several months, I no longer doubted God's love for me. There was no major event that influenced me, or an amazing sermon or book I received this assurance from, but from that point on, I have never doubted God's love for me. As I simply asked him over time, he blessed me with an assurance in my heart. I don't think this would have been possible if I had not already been working on false beliefs in my heart, so I believe I created the space for God to come in and make this assurance real in my heart. Even though I was telling others about Jesus, I think I would have eventually stopped telling others if I hadn't felt his love for me in my own heart. My identity and security in his love need to be stable and consistent in order for me to persevere in following Christ throughout my life.

4. Do offer to pray for people.

Even if I don't know what to say, praying for people can sometimes have an amazing impact on conversations that were limited. When a conversation with someone didn't really go anywhere or may have been difficult, toward the end I would ask, "Do you mind if I prayed for you now?" This is a risk but one worth taking if you're willing to set aside comfort in order to love someone else well.

After praying, people's countenance often changes. They often have not had people pray for them and they feel a sense of love and acceptance that sometimes eludes them when they just talk with people. I believe God meets us there in that moment and does what he loves to do—impart his love to others through our prayers for them.

Jesus once stated that we are to love our enemies. Even if we've never officially identified someone as an enemy, we all have them. And if you are going to be honest in a culture that's not okay with those who are different, then you are probably going to start developing connections with people who will hate you for your perspective.

This brings me to my last do.

5. Do expect that some people will reject you.

Paul faced this and wrote about it in the New Testament. Here's what he states in 1 Corinthians 1: "So when we preach that Christ was crucified, the Jews are offended and the Gentiles say it is all nonsense" (v. 23).

He states in Galatians 5 that he could preach a popular message that people wanted to hear regarding circumcision. At the time, some in the Galatian church were trying to lead the Jewish people back to the Old Testament belief that circumcision was one way to identify that you belonged to God.

But Paul was stating that their identity was solely and firmly in the death and resurrection of Jesus Christ on the cross. Here is what he states: "Dear brothers and sisters, if I were still preaching that you must be circumcised—as some say I do—why am I still being persecuted? If I were no longer preaching salvation through the cross of Christ, no one would be offended" (v. 11).

Paul is speaking to believers, not people who supposedly have no common belief with him. He is being challenged by people who profess to also believe in and follow Jesus. Regardless of where we are in conversations inside or outside the church, we will face people who don't agree. Some won't handle this disagreement well and might cut off relationship with you.

I've faced this many times over the course of my faith but more prominently in the past several years. Some of these were people whom I once considered friends. Their rejection has certainly been painful and causes me to grieve the losses. However, Jesus wants me to take my pain and grief to him:

> Now, who will want to harm you if you are eager to do good? But even if you suffer for doing what is right, God will reward you for it. So don't worry or be afraid of their threats. Instead, you must worship Christ as Lord of your life. And if someone asks about your Christian hope, always be ready to explain it. But do this in a gentle and respectful way. Keep your conscience clear. Then if people speak against you, they will be ashamed when they see what a good life you live because you belong to Christ. Remember, it is better to suffer for doing good, if that is what God wants, than to suffer for doing wrong! Christ suffered for our sins once for all time. He never sinned, but he died for sinners to bring you safely home to God. He suffered physical death, but he was raised to life in the Spirit. (1 Pet. 3:13–18)

Our encouragement through times of rejection is to remember what Jesus went through for you and me. He truly never did anything wrong but he died because I sinned and you sinned. He means for this to be encouraging to us, to remind us that we too can suffer like he did and he will be with us, eventually rewarding us for following him faithfully through difficult times.

Of course, in the early church, suffering often meant literally dying for your faith. Some Christians in the world still live under this danger today. We don't live under this kind of danger in the United States, but who's to say if that will change? Maybe someday we will face the same kind of persecution. Whether it's being rejected or literally giving our lives for our faith, Christ has gone before us and died in obedience to his heavenly Father. And he desires for us to follow him in this manner. As a son who has been loved so well by my Father in heaven, I can make this kind of commitment. This perspective helps me when troubles hit as I talk with people. Remember that Jesus loved you so much to die for you, and other people are worth the same kind of treatment as us.

14

Love Starts in the Family

A MOM WAS DABBING her eyes with a tissue, asking me, "What am I to do? I can't endorse his behavior. It's wrong. How am I supposed to feel hopeful when his future is in question? Will coming out as gay eventually kill him?" Her questions were out of fear, as she wondered if her son's involvement in gay relationships would result in him contracting HIV. Not knowing much about the gay community except for what she had heard from alarmists, her fears sometimes overtook her.

She and I had numerous conversations about her fears. I tried to correct false beliefs and miscommunication about the gay community. We prayed, hoping for her son to decide to give up pursuing a gay identity and find his peace in his relationship with Christ. She was not alone. Several other couples were sitting in the room, feeling the same pain, asking similar questions.

How was I to answer? My boys were still little, barely five and six years old. What did I know about children making life choices that could be permanent and send them in a totally different trajectory than what I hoped for them? These parents were facing this turmoil. As they looked to me for an answer, I paused. Should I say what I was really thinking? There might be a defensive reaction or I could hurt someone's feelings. Could it be that this question was from the Holy Spirit? I took the risk and asked the roomful of parents this question: "What sin would you be comfortable with your sons and daughters having?"

For five years, I ran a support group for parents of children who had come out as gay. I listened to these moms and dads express their confusion and pain over their sons and daughters. For many of them, having a son or daughter come out feels like a death sentence. Thoughts run wild. They wonder if their child's sexual behavior is out of control or managed. "Will my son contract a sexually transmitted disease?" "Is this a death sentence for the hope of seeing my daughter get married and have kids?" "I may never have grandkids." These thoughts and questions can dominate a parent's thoughts and impact how they relate to their children.

My question wasn't intended to dismiss or distract them from their pain. Underneath my question was the more important question of why they were reacting so strongly to their child stating that he or she was gay. Sleepless nights, bouts of crying, anger, and anxiety are not unusual symptoms for parents who don't know what to do with their child's declaration. I've seen parents be completely traumatized by, "Mom, Dad, I'm gay." Yet they don't seem to be nearly as troubled about their children being prejudiced or greedy.

I know there are parents who suffer and struggle with their children's sinful behavior that is not same-sex attraction. However, the parents in my group seemed different. They seemed isolated in their churches, in the same way that their children often felt isolated because of their confusion over sexual identity. They didn't feel they could share their struggles with other parents who had children the same age as theirs. The sin of *their* children was not viewed in the same manner as the sin of children with other struggles.

Why? What was *so horrible* about their child's sinful behavior that caused them to lose hope in Jesus and fail to see that the story is not over and God is still working?

After I asked my question, the parents did not know how to answer. They weren't sure as to why I was asking this question, so I explained myself. I took a breath and thought, "Here goes."

"Look, I don't want you to feel that I don't see your pain. I know this is very real to you and weighs heavily on your hearts. But, honestly, your children are going to struggle with some kind of sin because all of us do as humans. Would you struggle as much if your son was prideful or greedy? Would you stay awake at night, troubled that your daughter was racist or was unforgiving toward her siblings? Think about it. If you would not have the same reaction about your son or daughter's sin that wasn't homosexually related, then there is something wrong, because the last time I read the Bible, Jesus died on the cross because *all* sin separated us from God. So, your son and daughter are going to be battling some sin because they are human.

"And let's be even more honest, all of the sins I mentioned are rampant in the church and many Christians are not panicking at all about the fact that these sins are widespread. If we are more troubled by homosexuality than any other, then we are not thinking the way God thinks."

WHOM JESUS CONDEMNED

The church today has not thought the same way about all sin. To be true, certainly not all sin is the same in the sense that the *consequences* are different. Committing murder has much more serious consequences than shoplifting a piece of candy. In terms of eternal consequences, though, all sin keeps us from being perfect, the standard by which we enter heaven. Since no one can be perfect, we rely completely upon the death and resurrection of Jesus Christ.

I actually had one parent state that he believed homosexuality *was* worse than other sins. When I asked him to give some biblical support for this perspective, he couldn't quote one Bible verse. Nor did he give any other support for his position. I never did find out why he believed this to be true because he only came once to the support group, but I'm sure he represents a certain segment of Christians.

I want to be clear with you, readers, that *all* sin keeps us from God and it doesn't matter how good or bad the sin is from our perspective. Faith in Christ alone is what enables you and me to enter heaven. That's it.

Jesus made it very clear, also, how he felt about sin by what he modeled. Reading through the gospels, the individuals that Jesus was harshest with were the Pharisees. There was that moment with the tax collectors when Jesus turned over the tables and raised quite a stir. But, for the most part, the religious leaders were his targets for rebuke. They were, if you will, the "pastors" of the day: spiritual leaders who were supposed to lead the people in their relationship with God. Yet they were failing miserably. These were the only people Jesus called names: hypocrites, blind fools, brood of vipers, white-washed tombs (Matt 3:7, 15:3–9, 23; John 3:6–8). These insults might not sound like much to you, but back then these remarks were very offensive. Through Jesus' rebuke of the religious leaders, he was definitely conveying that they were *worse* than those whom they looked down upon, including tax collectors, prostitutes, and lepers. Jesus seemed to be more troubled by *religious* behavior than what we might call blatant sin. Religious behavior *is* sin.

By Jesus' life and example, we need to know how he lived and follow him. We need to study to make sure we understand what he said to the religious leaders and why, so we don't fall into the same trap. Jesus wasn't just talking to *those bad* religious leaders back when he was walking the earth. He was speaking to the Pharisees from every time period in history, including our country, in our time, right now.

Do you know what it means to be guilty of being a Pharisee? Study the gospels and notice their behavior and make sure that you do all you can to avoid looking, talking, and acting like a Pharisee. Many in the church today are guilty of being Pharisees in how they have related to those with same-sex attraction. Part of the reason some of the parents in my support group were struggling is that they battled the same kind of pharisaical spirit as the religious leaders did back in Jesus' day. Many of us are guilty of spiritual pride without even realizing it. We get exposed when we talk about the issue of homosexuality and start to think or say that this sin is worse than other sins.

Some Christians might pull out the verses that state homosexuality is an abomination (Lev. 18:22, 20:13, KJV). They will, however, neglect Proverbs 6:17–19, which states that there are seven sins that are an abomination to God: "a proud look, a lying tongue, and hands that shed innocent blood; an heart that deviseth wicked imaginations, feet that be swift in running to mischief, a false witness that speaketh lies, and he that soweth discord among brethren" (KJV).

To put it in modern language, the seven sins God hates are: "haughty eyes, a lying tongue, hands that kill the innocent, a heart that plots evil, feet that race to do wrong, a false witness who pours out lies, a person who sows discord in a family."

Looking at this list, I think a great many more of us would be guilty of committing "abominations." So, if we are going to put gays and lesbians in the abomination category, we need to do the same for the rest us on this list. Let's be consistent rather than hypocritical.

From my perspective, however, when Christ died on the cross for our sins and rose again, he took care of the condemnation for any abomination we would commit. The focus, as children of God, ceases to be on the behavior and is now present on our identity and call to remember that Christ resides within us. If we call ourselves his followers and love him, then our motivation to obey him is out of love, not to avoid any abomination list so we can *get good with God*.

Remember, we are not made right with God by good things we do or sin we avoid, but by faith in Christ alone (Rom. 3:28; Eph. 2:8–9; 2 Tim. 1:9; Titus 3:5–7). So when we commit *any* sin, we confess and are quickly forgiven, seeking to not commit those sins again so we don't continue to damage relationship with God and people. But if we do fail again, we are covered by Christ's blood, and we can get back up and keep trying because of his grace and mercy and all that he empowers us with to live a godly life.

I'm focusing on clarifying perspective on sin once again because it's imperative that you, as a family member of someone who is gay, have a right perspective on sin and on your own identity in Christ. If you don't, then you can't lead your loved one on a path in the right direction spiritually. You'll mislead them another false path that is opposite of the way they are walking but is still false. You'll be leading them down a religious path, rather than a path toward Christ and Christ-likeness, which is the ultimate goal.

SO, WHAT NOW?

My focus has been somewhat more on parents since the beginning of this chapter, but what I want to teach you is applicable to anyone, whether you are a parent, grandparent, aunt or uncle, sibling, cousin, or close friend. Even though there are unique aspects to each kind of relationship, let's begin with the foundation from which to build.

1. Learn to live in the present, day by day. Any other way of thinking and living is choosing to live in fantasy.

What do I mean by this? Often parents face fears that I mentioned at the beginning of the chapter, or thoughts and questions that stir up fear. However, these thoughts and questions are based upon trying to predict the future. Parents often live in fear because they have hopes that their children will get married and have children, and that may not happen now. Perhaps they've heard about AIDS and fear their child will contract the disease.

All of this thinking is fantasy thinking. None of these things have happened yet. Their children may never change in their sexual attractions but who knows if they will. Maybe they'll change their mind and decide that a gay identity is not what Christ desires for them. Maybe they *will* get married and have children. To try and look ahead to the future and play out in their minds what may or may not happen stirs up emotions that don't need to be present. Sometimes I call this thought process fortune-telling.

Allow me to visit, once again, the circumstance of my wife's diagnosis of leukemia. Her particular kind was a deadly form called acute lympho-blastic leukemia (ALL). When children get leukemia, they are typically diagnosed with this type. But for children, the chance of being healed is high, like 90 percent. For adults, however, being diagnosed with this type of leukemia is deadly, and many die from it. With my wife's particular risk factors, she was given a 20 percent chance of survival without a bone marrow transplant. The chance of survival was raised to 50 percent if she did get a bone marrow transplant.

Within two hours of the diagnosis, Laura was admitted to the hospital, and we were told she would be there for thirty days and that she could not work for a year. I began imagining selling our home because my wife made at least two-thirds of our household income and we could not survive on my income alone.

For two weeks, I cried myself to sleep. My thoughts gravitated, obviously, to my wife dying. How would my boys survive her death? How would we all survive her death? I went to my counselor, George, who really saved my life. My friends and family could understand why I was afraid; practically anyone can understand this type of fear. My counselor, however, challenged me on this thinking. He asked me, "What are you thinking about that causes you to be afraid?"

I said I was thinking about my wife dying and how it would impact all of us.

He asked, "Well, why are you thinking about her dying? Do you want her to die?"

Now I was getting irked. "Of course not!"

He responded, "Then why are you thinking about her dying?"

I didn't understand what he meant. Wasn't it all right for me to think about this and be afraid?

He then explained, "Brad, the reason I'm saying this is that your wife is alive today. She has every hope of living today. To think about her dying would be living in fantasy. You have today! Make that your focus each morning you get up. Live each day, one at a time, and put aside any thoughts about the future. Whenever you start to fear, ask yourself: Am I living in fantasy or reality?"

I had no idea that what I was trying to control my life. I wasn't trusting God; I was relying upon myself by trying to jump ahead into the future and diminish possible pain by preparing myself. The problem, however, was that I was adding an emotional weight that made living day-to-day unbearable sometimes.

No one was challenging me on my fantasy thinking. George was right! I didn't have to live in fear; I could live in the freedom of staying in the moment and being with the one I love, without fear of the future. If I had spent that year worrying every day, stressing myself horribly would have been a waste of time because the end of this story was awesome: my wife is alive today!

One example of how that emotional weight impacted how I related to others took place one morning after I dropped my boys off at school. I drove through a Starbucks drive-through before going to the hospital. After driving up to the window, the employee asked, "How are you doing today?"

"Horrible," I responded, only I didn't use such a nice word. (I used a word that's not appropriate to put in print.)

He asked, "Oh, how come? Are you having a bad morning?"

I flipped out! I unloaded on this poor soul. I yelled back, "Bad day! My wife is in the hospital with cancer and I don't know if she's going to live or die! I don't have the luxury of having a bad day!"

This poor young man backed up and said, "Oh, I'm so sorry." He handed me my drink and I drove off.

Most people would understand why I was under so much stress. Some people might even excuse my sinful behavior as being a result of *legitimate* emotional stress. However, Jesus *never* says it is okay for me to sin against people when I'm stressed. He actually never endorses living a life of fear and worry. In fact, he spoke this message to his disciples:

> That is why I tell you not to worry about everyday life—whether you have enough food and drink, or enough clothes to wear. Isn't life more than food, and your body more than clothing? Look at the birds. They don't plant or harvest or store food in barns, for your heavenly Father feeds them. And aren't you far more valuable to him than they are? Can all your worries add a single moment to your life?

And why worry about your clothing? Look at the lilies of the field and how they grow. They don't work or make their clothing, yet Solomon in all his glory was not dressed as beautifully as they are. And if God cares so wonderfully for wildflowers that are here today and thrown into the fire tomorrow, he will certainly care for you. Why do you have so little faith?

So don't worry about these things, saying, "What will we eat? What will we drink? What will we wear?" These things dominate the thoughts of unbelievers, but your heavenly Father already knows all your needs. Seek the Kingdom of God above all else, and live righteously, and he will give you everything you need.

So don't worry about tomorrow, for tomorrow will bring its own worries. Today's trouble is enough for today. (Matt. 6:25–34)

Today's trouble is enough for today! For over a year, my wife faced treatment for leukemia. Some days were difficult and some were lighter days. Through it all, though, I found that I actually had control over the thoughts I allowed to go through my mind. The more I disciplined myself to focus on the moment, the more the days were doable. I didn't always feel overwhelmed by the days. God was present, and we saw how much he provided for us throughout each week. My counselor taught me that a significant part of my emotional weight was how much I lived in fantasy in the future rather than in the moment right now.

After my wife was healed of leukemia, I applied the thinking I learned while she was ill. I never realized how much emotional weight I carried around by living in the future.

Each week now, if I start to feel anger or anxiety, I ask myself, "Am I living in fantasy or reality? Am I having imaginary conversations with people? Do I worry that my kids won't get sick and miss out on an important event? Are there people that I worry about because of the choices they have made, and am I worrying because I'm thinking about their future?"

These questions cause me to stop and set aside any thinking about the future and focus exclusively on the moment. I can't tell you how much it has not only relieved me of emotional weight but has enabled me to enjoy life more fully because I enjoy the moments *as I am experiencing them*: enjoying a good cup of Starbucks (yes, I'm a Starbucks addict); staying present with the friend with whom I'm having lunch; laughing at my kids' jokes; and listening to them when we are together. I don't waste any more energy thinking about tomorrow or the next day or the next month.

Each day really *does* have enough trouble of its own! Jesus actually *did* know what he was talking about! Sometimes I wonder if Jesus would be thrilled if we actually just *did* what he said rather than ignore or question it, like I have done many times.

I have certainly experienced the benefit of following his counsel and my hope is that you can too. Trusting God *is* the way to live and setting aside fantasy thinking is one way I trust him— by not trying to control the future; by not trying to protect myself from pain; and believing that if I need him for a difficult moment in the future, I can wait upon him to be there and provide for me.

Don't let your fears about your loved ones dominate your thinking so that you end up sinning against them by arguing with them, manipulating them, or trying to control their future or behavior. Let them be where they are in their journey without judgment or condemnation. Jesus never pressured anyone to follow him. He never hollered at them when they walked away from him, *"You're going to regret it! You'll wish you made the right decision later on!"* He let them be where they are in the journey, knowing that the story was not over.

That person is still alive. As long as they are living, there is always hope!

2. Don't focus on the behavior but on the true identity of the person.

Maybe your loved one wants to make his or her identity being gay, and his or her world is dominated by thinking about being gay and pointing out the prejudices against gay people, etc. However, you don't have to make that how you see them. Once again, everyone is a human being created in the image of God. Gender is part of an individual's identity but doesn't encompass someone completely. Sexual desires are certainly not used to define a person, according to Jesus. We insult each other by reducing our identity to sexual desires, making that a significant part of who we are. Living out true biblical masculinity and femininity is certainly an important part of our identity, but we must always remember that we are human beings first, created in the image of God, and that gives us value. We are not valued first because we are male or female, straight or gay.

You can contribute to your loved one's preoccupation with being gay by having that dominate your thoughts as well. Did you love that person before he or she came out as gay? What did you enjoy about his or her personality and talents prior to their living as a gay man or lesbian? How can you continue to relate to them in a similar manner, such that not their sexuality but who they truly are is the primary reference point?

Help your loved ones think more complexly about themselves by expanding beyond *their* primary reference point as being gay. Some people are preoccupied with being gay because they are insecure at heart and having an identity of some kind feels safer than not knowing who you are or where you fit in. The goal is to help them understand that they don't need to *fit in*. The goal is to affirm their uniqueness and help them be who they truly are (not being gay but the essence of who they are as the one you love), so they can be celebrated for that uniqueness rather than pressured to fit in with a category or group of people.

Learn to know your loved one. Maybe there's more to this person than you have ever thought about before. He or she came out and some of you were shocked by this revelation. Obviously you don't know your loved one as well as you think, so the focus can be more on truly knowing him or her. As we've spoken before, the way to earn trust or maintain trust in a relationship is to ask questions and listen.

John Moe is an American writer and reporter. I saw his quote one year when Starbucks (yes, Starbucks again!) printed quotes on their cups from famous (and not-so-famous) people. I liked what John said: "You can learn a lot more from listening than you can from talking. Find someone with whom you don't agree in the slightest and ask them to explain themselves at length. Then take a seat, shut your mouth, and don't argue back. It's physically impossible to listen with your mouth open."

As you listen, you'll learn things you never knew before. One simple question is to ask your loved ones to share the journey of how they came to understand they are gay. Most people have a difficult emotional journey coming to this conclusion, and then coming out to people, when they may be rejected or abandoned for their decision, is a big hurdle. It is not an easy journey and someone needs to hear their story.

Hopefully as they share, you'll listen well and the conversation will elicit more questions to ask, so that you may know your loved ones better than ever before. Should a time come for you to share with them or speak into their lives, you will be much more effective with your words because you will know this person better.

So many Christians relate to people based upon formulaic thoughts rather than unique, specific statements that can be applied much more effectively to an individual. A healthier and spiritually mature way to love others is not to go by generalities but to look for uniqueness. As we've mentioned before, Jesus related very uniquely to people rather than living under generalities.

Our willingness to listen well not only applies to our loved ones but also to the Holy Spirit. As we listen to him, he will lead us in what to say or ask. With some people, I don't even share my point of view. Sometimes I just ask questions and individuals can confuse themselves by their own thought processes. Most of us don't even realize how we contradict ourselves by what we say or how we live.

The sad truth is that most people don't care enough to work hard at relationships. By being people who are willing to ask questions and listen, we can become a safe place that opens doors to talk more honestly. These moments can become times of sharing what is true.

The goal, however, is *not* to get to what *you* want to say! The goal is to truly know and love the person. Let God do the revealing as to the right time to speak. We usually want to jump way ahead of the game in telling the truth. That's some of our fortune-telling playing out. We want to jump ahead for a reason, and it's not usually focused on trusting God for the right time or truly caring for our loved ones, but it's more about our discomfort with their gay identity.

3. Pray for your loved one.

Can we do anything better than pray faithfully for our loved ones? The door may not be open for our loved ones to listen to us. Perhaps they have cut off relationship rather than listen to you, and you feel the pain strongly. God cares about how you feel. He cares about your longing for your loved one. Praying will help heal your wounds and strengthen you for the journey that may be longer than expected.

But who prays faithfully for people? I don't know anyone who can pray more passionately or fervently for someone other than those who love that person. So many people I know, who have come out of living as a gay man or lesbian, had a loved one praying faithfully for them. God reaches out to people even when there is no opportunity to speak into that person's life.

Let me share an example. When I was doing ministry in Chicago, one week a young man came to the church office where I counseled people. After we were introduced, we sat down and he shared about his journey.

For years, he had battled same-sex attraction and decided to come out and live as a gay man. He was in a relationship with a man for a couple of years. He worked at a business that was owned by gay people. His family was gay-affirming and his church was gay-affirming.

However, as he was reading the Bible one time, he came upon some Scriptures that stated that homosexuality was wrong. At that moment, he felt conviction from the Holy Spirit. He spoke to his pastor about these passages, and the pastor explained that these verses are not accurately interpreted and do not refer to loving, same-sex relationships. The pastor then pointed out that he was possibly experiencing homophobic feelings from the culture and the traditional church that have been projected unto him, and he was allowing those feelings to influence his thoughts.

This young man was not convinced. He knew that how he was living was not right. No one in his world supported him in his perspective, so he left his church, job, and partner, and came to our church looking for answers consistent with his convictions. I shared with him my perspective and my testimony, and he ended up staying and going through counseling to face what in his life needed to be addressed.

I share this to encourage you that just because someone is isolated from you and others who differ from a gay-affirming perspective, that does not mean the Holy Spirit has stopped working. God works whether that person is seeking the Lord or not, and your prayers can be a significant part of softening that person's heart to receive the truth when he or she is ready. Some doors can only be opened by prayer (Mark 9:14–28; Col. 4:2–4).

Now, this is not a magic elixir that will cause everyone you pray for to become open to a traditional Christian view on homosexuality. Some loved ones will still identify as gay or lesbian. We don't have control over anyone's life, ever. We can pray and then share the truth when the Holy Spirit opens the door.

Which reminds me, I need to encourage you that sometimes your prayers are more for you than for the other person. Our praying is not meant to be used to get from God what we want, for ourselves or others. Our praying is part of our relationship with God, where we entrust to him all of our thoughts and feelings, believing that he loves us and wants us to know him.

I have spoken to Christians who really don't see the point of prayer when prayers are not always answered as they want them to be. They ask, "Why should I pray if God knows what I need and does what he wants anyway?" The purpose is for relationship with God, to know him and to submit your heart to him so that he can create in you a heart for him. This is the confidence we have in approaching God: that if we ask anything *according to his will*, he hears us (1 John 5:14). The more time you spend talking to him, the more you will have his heart in yours. So, when you're praying for your loved one, remember that God is working in your heart as well.

If you aren't praying over your sinful behavior more than for your loved one's sin, you are missing the mark, from my perspective. We must first always see our sin as worse if we are to have an accurate perspective about bringing others before the throne. Our loved ones *know* if we think our sin is not as bad as theirs. We need to model that we are just as concerned about the state of our own relationship with God as we are about their relationship with God. Their relationship with God is not more important than your own. They are equally valuable, and as you work on your own heart, you will know how to better love your child, your sister, your brother, your grandchildren, your cousin, and your friend.

I think the gay community is looking and longing for someone to model for them what it's like to live a life of transparency and full disclosure before God, allowing him to transform every aspect of your life. They don't want to see Christians just pointing out how they are getting it wrong.

Now, your loved one is just as immature as we can be in how we relate to them. We would obviously like them to relate to us maturely as well, but we must always ask first: Does our loved one have a relationship with Jesus? If not, then it's inappropriate for us to expect any kind of godly behavior. It's difficult enough to live out godly behavior with the power of the Spirit within us. But for those who do not follow God, the Scriptures say they are slaves to sin:

> Because of the weakness of your human nature, I am using the illustration of slavery to help you understand all this. Previously, you let yourselves be slaves to impurity and lawlessness, which led ever deeper into sin. Now you must give yourselves to be slaves to righteous living so that you will become holy. When you were slaves to sin, you were free from the obligation to do right. And what was the result? You are now ashamed of the things you used to do, things that end in eternal doom. But now you are free from the power of sin and have become slaves of God. Now you do those things that lead to holiness and result in eternal life. (Rom. 6:19–22)

So, the priority in this circumstance is to focus on leading someone to know Jesus Christ. There's no reason to address any kind of same-sex behavior or relationship if there is no commitment to Christ.

4. Shift from the perspective of a biological family to a spiritual family.

What do I mean by this statement? Some people, especially parents, are vulnerable to always praying and waiting for their loved ones to finally give up living as gay people and follow Christ's path for them sexually. Weighed down with emotions, they can obsess about just caring for one's own children and one's own family.

However, American Christians have often misunderstood the biblical concept of *family*. Family, from a biblical perspective, is not about the biological family but the larger spiritual family. We have Scriptures to support the concept of spiritual adoption.

First, we are adopted by God into the Kingdom. Paul speaks of this in Romans 8: "So you have not received a spirit that makes you fearful slaves. Instead, you received God's Spirit when he adopted you as his own children. Now we call him, 'Abba, Father.' For his Spirit joins with our spirit to affirm that we are God's children. And since we are his children, we are his heirs. In fact, together with Christ we are heirs of God's glory. But if we are to share his glory, we must also share his suffering" (vv. 15–17).

This has always been God's desire. King David spoke of this in Psalm 68 when he wrote, "Father to the fatherless, defender of widows—this is God, whose dwelling is holy. God places the lonely in families; he sets the prisoners free and gives them joy" (vv. 5–6).

He is creating a new family, a new kingdom where no one is left out. No one is abandoned in God's kingdom. Part of our encouragement is that we are to see that we have a new life ahead, a new hope in which we have an inheritance awaiting us (Rom. 8:23–25).

Jesus also modeled this life of the new spiritual family. "As Jesus was speaking to the crowd, his mother and brothers stood outside, asking to speak to him. Someone told Jesus, 'Your mother and your brothers are outside, and they want to speak to you.' Jesus asked, 'Who is my mother? Who are my brothers?' Then he pointed to his disciples and said, 'Look, these are my mother and brothers. Anyone who does the will of my Father in heaven is my brother and sister and mother!'" (Matt. 12:46–50).

The family is now expanded to anyone who does the will of the Father, not just to those who are biologically related. He assures us that if we face the pain of losing biological family because they do not agree with us following Jesus, he comforts us with the perspective of a larger family: "I assure you that everyone who has given up house or brothers or sisters or mother or father or children or property, for my sake and for the Good News, will receive now in return a hundred times as many houses, brothers, sisters, mothers, children, and property—along with persecution. And in the world to come that person will have eternal life. But many who are the greatest now will be least important then, and those who seem least important now will be the greatest then" (Mark 10:29–31).

Jesus comforted his own biological family while on the cross. When John and Mary, the mother of Jesus, were standing at the foot of the cross, the following took place: "Standing near the cross were Jesus' mother, and his mother's sister, Mary (the wife of Clopas), and Mary Magdalene. When Jesus saw his mother standing there beside the disciple he loved, he said to her, 'Dear woman, here is your son.' And he said to this disciple, 'Here is your mother.' And from then on this disciple took her into his home" (John 19:25–27). He was assuring Mary that she had a spiritual family, one that would take care of her.

One theory is that Jesus' half-brothers didn't really believe in him until after he resurrected. Joseph, the husband of Mary, had died and was not there to care for her. Jesus, as the eldest son, was dying and was responsible to care for his mother. He loved her and made sure that she was cared for by someone who was not only a relative but, more importantly, was a son of God in the kingdom of God.

Some of you have loved ones who identify as gay and there seems to be no evidence that this will change in the near future. However, there are spiritual brothers and sisters in the church right now who desire to address this issue in their lives. They believe acting on their same-sex desires is not in line with God's plan for their lives. They are seeking help and support, and someone to reach out to them while they face this struggle. What prevents you from being available for these individuals who are your brothers and sisters?

For some of you parents, these can be your spiritual sons and daughters. You can offer them encouragement, hope, and support in the midst of their struggles. Seeking to overcome same-sex attraction can be a difficult journey, and they need all the prayer and support they can get.

In addition to praying for and supporting those who desire to work on their same-sex attraction issues, you need to ask yourself if your church is a safe place for people coming out of homosexuality to attend. I've had some parents tell me that their church is not a safe place to struggle with this issue. *They* didn't feel comfortable even asking for prayer from people at church for their children. If that's the case, then your work is to get involved in making your church a safe place. Why would you want your loved one to come out of homosexuality if the church is not a safe place for them to go?

Do what you can to learn about and understand the issue of same-sex attraction. Offer to teach your spiritual leaders in your church about this issue, or teach a Sunday school class. There are steps you can take to make sure that if your sons or daughters were to come to your church, they would feel safe and supported. Even if your loved one doesn't live in the same area as you, you are still helping the church as a whole continue to grow and mature by developing your church into a safe place in your town or city. You can be part of helping the church mature by exchanging the focus of the biological family for the spiritual family, where all are valued and esteemed.

Some of you still have questions about how to love your loved one. This question is often asked: During holidays, should I let my child come home with his or her partner and stay in our home?

These kinds of questions are not always going to be answered by a formula. I know this may be what some of you desire, but you have to be willing to allow God to speak to you about your own situation. What applies to one person or family does not apply to another. I've had one set of parents ask that their son stay somewhere else with his partner, while another set of parents allows their daughter to stay with them along with her partner. I don't judge either parent for their decision. The most important thing is how you sense God leading you in your relationship with your child or your loved one. It doesn't always have to look the same way. We need to move away from formulas and learn how to rely upon the Holy Spirit's leading as we face these situations.

And be willing to make a mistake! Is there no forgiveness with God? As a believer, are we no longer condemned for any sinful behavior? God knows we are confused by situations and circumstances sometimes. We can't always get it right. That's why Jesus died on the cross, so whether we know we are sinning or not, our sin is covered under the blood of Christ. There is no condemnation anymore. Let yourself make a mistake with God and with people. Keep praying and seeking his heart. He will lead you if you trust him rather than relying upon formulaic ways of relating. There is tons of grace with God. Remember, he *loves* you more than you will ever know! He's already proven it through Jesus. Trust him!

15

The Journey Out

AFTER FIVE YEARS OF working on his unwanted same-sex attractions, Dakwon continues to ask himself, "Why do I continue to struggle with these attractions?' He faithfully attends church, regularly reads his Bible, and prays, asking God to deliver him from these unwanted desires. Attending support groups each week and going to counseling has helped him come out of his depression and not battle anxiety as much. He enjoys his friendships more and grows in his ability to be more transparent. The nagging question, however, still exists: why?

In the previous chapters, I have addressed the complexity of developing same-sex attractions. Easy, simple solutions do not exist for such a journey in overcoming desires. Expecting the journey to be simple is a major weakness in individuals and the church. Once we arrive at this understanding of the complexity of same-sex attractions, the process of addressing this issue will be equally complex. Talking about this in one chapter would be ludicrous. There are entire books dedicated to this lengthy process. What I would like to do instead is share with you, as the reader, three crucial aspects of understanding how to minister to one another, including those with same-sex attraction. Perhaps this can elicit a more compassionate response toward those addressing same-sex issues in their lives. As a result, we can be properly led to help someone who struggles, asking, "What part can I play in helping my brothers and sisters who are struggling?"

"This is not a twenty-five-weeks-and-you're-straight program."

Another one of my support groups began around ten years ago. Participants sat in the room quietly, not looking at each other but staring straight ahead to the front of the room. The leadership team had just finished praying. One of the young men I had previously met and invited to join this group approached me outside the entrance to the room. As we were speaking, I got the sense he was hoping that, by the end of the program, he would be completely free from his same-sex attractions.

These words came out of my mouth: "John, this is not a twenty-five-weeks-and-you're-straight program."

His countenance fell and his face became sullen. "I thought I would be free from this by the end of the program." He stayed for the night but never came back or spoke to me again.

Was this wrong for me to say? How could it be wrong for me to say if it is true? One of the illusions in our culture and the church is that we can overcome complicated problems fairly quickly. If we don't see quick success, something must be wrong with the method. I certainly understand the desire for a quick fix solution. I've desired this for my own life. If I had a pill to give anyone who wanted to change their sexual desires, I would be selling them left and right. I would be rich, and people wanting change would be thrilled.

However, God did not call us into relationship so that he could fix my problems and I could get on with the way I think life should be. God calls us to die to ourselves completely, renouncing our own desires and plans in exchange for his will.

Some Christians will jump to Paul's perspective in 2 Corinthians 12 where Paul states that he asked God three times to deliver him from something and God refused. Instead God spoke to him about his grace being sufficient for him and that his power is perfected in weakness. I agree that this is certainly true. At the same time, I believe this Scripture is sometimes used to dismiss the complexity of working on our souls. Because we often function at an infant- or child-level of relational understanding, we are typically unaware of the process of working on deeper issues of the heart. God did not intend for this verse to be used in place of the hard work of healing. He intended it to be used when all else has failed, giving us an alternative to just giving up on him.

Paul had been through quite a bit of difficulty. 2 Corinthians 6:5–10 speaks of the challenges Paul faced:

We have been beaten, been put in prison, faced angry mobs, worked to exhaustion, endured sleepless nights, and gone without food. We prove ourselves by our purity, our understanding, our patience, our kindness, by the Holy Spirit within us, and by our sincere love. We faithfully preach the truth. God's power is working in us. We use the weapons of righteousness in the right hand for attack and the left hand for defense. We serve God whether people honor us or despise us, whether they slander us or praise us. We are honest, but they call us impostors. We are ignored, even though we are well known. We live close to death, but we are still alive. We have been beaten, but we have not been killed. Our hearts ache, but we always have joy. We are poor, but we give spiritual riches to others. We own nothing, and yet we have everything.

Most of us in the United States haven't experienced this kind of spiritual journey. We have troubles and struggles, but most of us haven't been beaten for our faith or gone through starvation because we are traveling and seeking to share the gospel with those who don't know about it. When Paul talks about asking God to remove a thorn from his side, this is in the context of his living a sacrificial life fraught with pains and suffering.

Can we honestly say that most of us are asking God this question after we have lived this kind of life? My guess is that very few, if any, of us can say this for ourselves. So let's keep perspective and remember that, once we have walked a path facing lots of challenges in our faith, *then* and only then should we consider 2 Corinthians 12 as our perspective.

Until then, there is work to do and most of it will take quite a bit of time. When I share that it took me ten years to experience a complete change in my life, most people feel discouraged. This, however, is only discouraging if you have the perspective that life *should* normally be easier. If you have an understanding that life is mostly difficult and challenging, you will see your work on your soul as being the normal process of life when dealing with something deeply embedded in your soul.

"In order to overcome this struggle, you must change how you think about everything and change how you live."

Wow! This seems drastic and harsh. However, the reality is that same-sex attractions develop from being wounded in relationship (as we have explained in the previous chapters) and our responses to this wounding set us up for these attractions. In order to lay an axe to the roots of same-sex attraction, we have to be willing to question our thought processes, our beliefs, and our sinful responses to our own stories. Sexual struggles are always the manifestation of deeper sins that have been committed long before these desires develop. This is true not only for the individual with same-sex attraction but also for those who battle heterosexual desires that are out of control.

I became friends with Richard a long time ago after spending time counseling him over the phone. Richard commented about one of the first times we talked. He stated that he never forgot how I asked him how he sinned against people each week.

Spending time reflecting on this can be quite challenging because it also requires feedback from those with whom we have friendships and relationships. Long before sexual struggles manifested, there were sinful choices to not trust others, to be passive-aggressive in response to being hurt in relationships, to exhibit little smirks when looking down upon others to feel better about ourselves. These behaviors are just some of the myriad of sinful behaviors we act out in relationships. Sinful behaviors are a great way of not dealing with our wounds because we are protecting ourselves. Sinful behaviors are a diversion from hurts within.

Preceding sinful behaviors are false beliefs we have developed in response to our wounding. To find freedom from sin, we must tackle the internal dialogue that goes on in our minds or the foundational beliefs that have shaped us.

When I was four years old, my infant brother died from a heart defect. I loved my brother. Still present in my mind are vivid memories of looking at him over the car seat as he came home from the hospital. Holding him and feeding him a bottle was another one of my cherished memories. Then there is the painful memory of my mother coming into the home, crying because he had died.

One night shortly after his death, as I was striving to fall asleep, I started to cry, thinking of my brother. I cried out for my mom. She came into the room, asking why I was crying.

"I'm crying about Brian."

"Oh!" was her response as she walked out of the room, leaving me alone with my feelings.

Anger flooded my heart as I wrestled with confusion as to why my mother would abandon me at that moment. From that time on, I changed how I responded to my mother and to life in general.

When I revisited this memory through prayer with a good friend, we identified two lies that were planted in my mind at that moment:

1. Your feelings are too much for people.
2. You have to face these feelings alone.

For three decades, I took the lens of these two lies and carried them around, filtering life experiences through them. How did this play out? My behavior changed, as I didn't seek to share my thoughts and feelings with my parents. When I faced rejection and abuse from peers in school, as well as confusion over my sexual desires, my parents were not where I went to for help. I went to no one and thus reaffirmed the belief that I had to handle my feelings and experiences on my own.

In earlier chapters, I already addressed how the suppression of emotions always results in the development of struggles (i.e. having same-sex attractions or other kinds of sexual struggles). In order for me to find progress in overcoming same-sex attractions, I had to die to these lies and live differently. In other words, I learned to identify my emotions, communicate them appropriately to others, and thus find support for what I was facing.

The beliefs I developed might seem ridiculous, but you have to remember that these were the beliefs of a four-year-old. Four-year-olds make these kinds of decisions. Now is a good time to remember that children are great observers but they are poor interpreters. I believe Paul alludes to this in 1 Corinthians 13:11 when he says, "When I was a child, I spoke and thought and reasoned as a child. But when I grew up, I put away childish things." All of us have developed false beliefs in response to the traumas we experience as children. We wrongly interpret these circumstances and develop beliefs that shape our behavior at a very early age.

I believe Paul calls us to maturity by setting aside childish things. What are these childish things? The way we used to think, reason, and speak. For those with unwanted same-sex attractions, a significant part of the healing process requires revisiting their own history of experiences and identifying what beliefs developed as a result.

Some of these experiences (because of their severity) and subsequent false beliefs have been forgotten and may only be retrieved through the work of the Holy Spirit. For anyone confused about why it's difficult to make progress with sexual struggles, this process alone can be lengthy and difficult. Not working on false beliefs will certainly prevent any kind of hope for healing.

"Overcoming sexual struggles requires a transformation of the way Americans view relationship with God and people."

Perhaps this statement comes across as overly dramatic or drastic. Maybe you think I'm being rather negative in my view of the American culture.

One of the common themes among the men I have counseled is the concept of disappointment in relationships with the same gender, especially in the context of church. Initially my belief was that this was a result of our "neediness" in wanting more from relationships because of being relationally starved in our family contexts. However, through my friendships with men from other countries and cultures, I have come to understand that Americans have a rather unique view of relationships. Rather than having a lifelong perspective on friendship, Americans view relationships as disposable.

In one of my many conversations with friends, one friend from India asked me about male friendships. With an almost angry countenance, he asked why Americans treat friendships so poorly, using the word *disposable* specifically. In India, he stated, when you are friends, you are friends for life.

In the midst of our conversation, his father interrupted to ask him something in their language. The conversation appeared heated, as my friend "went off" a bit on his father. At least that is how it appeared to me. After they finished this interaction, my friend just picked up in the conversation where we left off, as if nothing significant had taken place.

When I've seen heated debates between Americans, the relationship would end or there would be a silence between the individuals for a period of time. What fascinated me was that, in my home, this type of conversation was never allowed. And yet it seemed to be a normal part of life for this family. Could it be that conflict was accepted as a normal part of relationships for these individuals and that it exposed the weaknesses of our culture, in which conflict is handled poorly or avoided?

Over the course of the past two decades, I've challenged my thinking on how I view relationships and what my family, culture, and church communities have taught me. There is a profound difference in how Americans relate as opposed to many other cultures in the world. I'm not convinced that we've figured out relationship well.

I've heard many spiritual leaders refer to the individualism of our culture and how it differs from the concept of community in the kingdom of

God. Yet I see few willing to let go of this individualism. How we run our church programs and services very much reflects our individualism and separateness. There seems to be a difficulty in letting go of things we don't even believe in.

Jean Vanier has focused a lot on community, reflecting on the difficulty of dying to individualism: "Community is a place of conflict: conflict inside each of us. There is first of all the conflict between the values of the world and the values of community, between togetherness and independence. It is painful to lose one's independence, and to come into togetherness—not just proximity—to make decisions together, and not all alone. Loss of independence is painful, particularly in a world where we have been told to be independent and to cultivate the feeling that 'I don't need anyone else.'"[1] Donald Miller, in his book *Blue Like Jazz*, beautifully explains how I believe all of us struggle:

> Life was a story about me because I was in every scene. In fact, I was the only one in every scene. I was everywhere I went. If somebody walked into my scene, it would frustrate me because they were disrupting the general theme of the play, namely my comfort or glory . . . Living in community made me realize one of my faults: I was addicted to myself. All I thought about was myself. The only thing I really cared about was myself. I had very little concept of love, altruism, or sacrifice. I discovered that my mind is like a radio that picks up only one station, the one that plays me: *K-DON, all Don, all the time.*[2]

Perhaps we all struggle with what Miller shared because we are completely unaware of how much we are impacted by our own individualism, which feeds the selfishness that is so natural to our human nature. Jesus said, "There is no greater love than to lay down one's life for one's friends" (John 15:13). I'm not sure many of us even know what that means. Most of us are annoyed when we have to get out of bed at night to help a friend who needs comfort or encouragement. We'll make a meal for our friends when they are struggling, but we often won't inconvenience ourselves in ways that lasts for days, weeks, perhaps months.

My friend Richard has broken a few bones in his life while enjoying fun activities like skiing. When he broke his shoulder, he shared with me how friends would often bring a meal but no one would come to take his

1. Vanier, *From Brokenness to Community*, 30–31.
2. Miller, *Blue Like Jazz*, 180–181. Italics in original text.

garbage can out for him or iron his shirts and help him get dressed in the morning.

Folks, this is not difficult love. Jesus modeled love that reflects maturity: dying for a friend. Jesus modeled dying for us in hopes that we wouldn't restrict this experience to just him.

> Don't be selfish; don't try to impress others. Be humble, thinking of others as better than yourselves. Don't look out for your own interests, but take an interest in others. You *must have the same attitude that Christ Jesus had*. Though he was God, he did not think of equality with God as something to cling to. Instead, he gave up his divine privileges; he took the humble position of a slave and was born as a human being. When he appeared in human form, he humbled himself in obedience to God and died a criminal's death on a cross. (Phil. 2:3–8)[3]

My contention is that one of the main reasons we battle sexual struggles is that we do not have a healthy understanding of emotional intimacy: intimacy between parents and children, intimacy between husbands and wives, intimacy between same-sex friends, and intimacy in our church communities. We haven't bought into Jesus' way of loving and do not live sacrificial lives of loving others. Until we are willing to learn how to love the way Jesus modeled, we will continue to be overcome by many of our fleshly battles, including same-sex attraction.

One of the reasons people have same-sex attractions is because they haven't experienced the healthy physical and emotional intimacy that should take place in normal relationships between family and friends (especially in same-sex relationships) long before they enter any romantic love. I believe that same-sex attractions can exist in other cultures for the same reason as well as differing reasons because of cultural variations in relationships.

One of the love languages of Noah, my younger son, is physical touch. When I showed Noah the list of Type A and Type B traumas, he circled the trauma about not receiving enough physical affection. I trusted his response because I believed his explanations for circling the various traumas made total sense. However, I was still puzzled by his selection of physical touch.

My father rarely, if ever, gave me physical affection growing up. By the time I was an adolescent, I was craving physical affection. I believe one of

---

3. Italics added.

the reasons men struggle sexually in our culture is that they are starved in the area of physical touch. Sometimes the only way males receive physical affection is through having sex with someone or being sexual in other ways.

Since my father didn't touch me much, I committed to loving my sons differently. I hugged and kissed them every day, even into adolescence. Noah often sat on my lap while watching a movie. If anyone was going to lean or lie on me while sitting in the living room, it would be Noah. Sharing a hug is still a regular part of our relationship.

So what would cause him to circle that he lacked in this area? The explanation is that even though I did a good job of providing physical affection as a father, he needed more than I provided. My older son, Micah, didn't circle that trauma. My younger son, however, did. So Micah's physical affection needs were met by me, but Noah needed more. This is an example of the complexity of relationships and how you cannot relate to different people in the same way.

True relationship involves knowing someone well, understanding them in such a way that we can accurately meet their needs. Each relationship has varying levels of need, even in the common areas of needs. Our responsibility, as followers of Jesus, is to learn how to focus on our own needs but also become experts at the second greatest commandment: loving our neighbor as ourselves.

My understanding is that obedience to the first and second greatest commandments will take me a lifetime. Even then I'm not convinced I'll perfect it. This is my journey. I'll know I'm finished when my life looks like Jesus' life, and those that I love can give the feedback that I am loving them well.

Perhaps I'm being too simplistic in thinking that loving one another well can significantly help overcome same-sex-attraction struggles. However, over my two decades of experience, I have seen many men progress significantly in their journeys, partly because they have changed their life to include relationships that model healthy physical and emotional intimacy.

Try this in your communities. Feel free to share with me how I may be wrong on this matter. I'm happy to be wrong, but my sense is that you will be experiencing more of what Christ called us to, and this will bring major transformation to your spiritual communities.

Conclusion

THREE YEARS HAVE GONE by since I began the journey of writing this book. Many experiences and conversations have taken place since then. As I read through what I've written yet one more time, my beliefs have not changed. If anything, I have become more solidified in what I believe.

However, this book is still deficient. Further understanding is needed. In addition, what I have not given you is guidance on how to live out relationships intimately in the body of Christ.

This book is the first step in helping you gain a little bit more understanding of the complex matter of same-sex attraction. Continuing to grow further in your understanding will require living out new concepts explained in this book. It's not enough to understand something intellectually. There must be experiences to solidify in our hearts what we believe with our minds.

The next book, perhaps, will focus on how to do relationship in a way that is closer to the kingdom of God than where we are now. Taking on this challenge feels a bit overwhelming to me because I'm still in the middle of learning how to love Jesus' way. I could not possibly presume to be an expert on this matter.

Who can be *the* expert on the matter of loving well? Perhaps none of us individually, but collectively, there have to be some Christian communities in this country that can model for us a more accurate experience of loving in God's way. Are you willing to take up the mantle and ask Jesus to enable you and your church or spiritual community to love like him? Would you more intentionally enter the realm of loving those with same-sex attractions? No one has to be an expert to learn how to love. You and I just need a willing heart, and Jesus will teach you as he has led me well all these years.

Many authors have gone before me, explaining varying aspects of same-sex attraction. I have included them at the end of this book. My prayer is that you will continue to read more, pray more, and engage with those who understand from personal experience what it's like to be sexually drawn to the same gender. Understanding my own story and sharing in the stories of many others wasn't just a journey into clarity on sexual struggles. This was a journey of understanding the human heart and what we all need in our relationships with Jesus Christ and one another.

Thank you for allowing me to share what I believe with you. Feel free to engage in conversation with me about these concepts. Through our journey together in the body of Christ, I know we can arrive at God's calling for our lives in living out the first and second greatest commandments.

Further Reading on Same-Sex Attraction

Bergner, Mario. *Setting Love in Order: Hope and Healing for the Homosexual.* Grand Rapids, MI: Baker, 1995.

Comiskey, Andrew. *Naked Surrender: Coming Home to Our True Sexuality.* Downers Grove, IL: InterVarsity, 2010.

Dallas, Joe. *Desires in Conflict: Hope for Men Who Struggle with Sexual Identity.* Eugene, OR: Harvest House, 1991.

————. *The Gay Gospel?: How Pro-Gay Advocates Misread the Bible.* Eugene, OR: Harvest House, 2007.

————. *When Homosexuality Hits Home: What to Do When a Loved One Says They're Gay.* Eugene, OR: Harvest House, 2004.

Dallas, Joe, and Nancy Heche. *The Complete Christian Guide to Understanding Homosexuality: A Biblical and Compassionate Response to Same-Sex Attraction.* Eugene, OR: Harvest House, 2010.

Davies, Bob, and Lela Gilbert. *Portraits of Freedom: 14 People Who Came Out of Homosexuality.* Downers Grove, IL: InterVarsity, 2001.

Gagnon, Robert A. J. *The Bible and Homosexual Practice: Texts and Hermeneutics.* Nashville: Abingdon, 2001.

Haley, Mike. *101 Frequently Asked Questions about Homosexuality.* Eugene, OR: Harvest House, 2004.

Hallman, Janelle M. *The Heart of Female Same-Sex Attraction: A Comprehensive Counseling Resource.* Downers Grove, IL: InterVarsity, 2008.

Howard, Jeanette. *Into the Promised Land: Beyond the Lesbian Struggle.* Oxford: Monarch, 2005.

Johnson, Kristin. *Sexual Wholeness in a Broken World.* OneByOne, 2008.

Jones, Stanton L., and Mark A. Yarhouse. *Ex-gays?: A Longitudinal Study of Religiously Mediated Change in Sexual Orientation.* Downers Grove, IL: IVP Academic, 2007.

Lerner, Robert, and Althea K. Nagai. *No Basis: What the Studies Don't Tell Us About Same-Sex Parenting.* Washington, DC: Marriage Law Project, 2001.

Medinger, Alan P. *Growth into Manhood: Resuming the Journey.* Colorado Springs, CO: Waterbrook, 2000.

Nicolosi, Joseph. *Reparative Therapy of Male Homosexuality: A New Clinical Approach.* Northvale, NJ: Jason Aronson, 1991.

Paulk, Anne. *Restoring Sexual Identity: Hope for Women Who Struggle with Same-Sex Attraction.* Eugene, OR: Harvest House, 2003.

Payne, Leanne. *The Broken Image: Restoring Personal Wholeness through Healing Prayer.* Westchester, IL: Cornerstone, 1981.

Thompson, Chad W. *Loving Homosexuals as Jesus Would: A Fresh Christian Approach.* Grand Rapids, MI: Brazos, 2004.

Worthen, Anita, and Bob Davies. *Someone I Love Is Gay: How Family & Friends Can Respond.* Downers Grove, IL: InterVarsity, 1996.

Yarhouse, Mark A. *Homosexuality and the Christian: A Guide for Parents, Pastors, and Friends.* Bloomington, MN: Bethany House, 2010.

Bibliography

Allender, Dan B., and Tremper Longman. *The Cry of the Soul: How Our Emotions Reveal Our Deepest Questions about God*. Colorado Springs, CO: NavPress, 1994.

American Psychological Association. "Sexual Orientation and Homosexuality: Answers to Your Questions for a Better Understanding." http://www.apa.org/topics/lgbt/orientation.aspx.

Arthur, Kay. *Lord, I Want to Know You: A Devotional Study of the Names of God*. Colorado Springs, CO: WaterBrook, 2000.

Bailey, J. Michael, and Richard C. Pillard. "A Genetic Study of Male Sexual Orientation," *Archives of General Psychiatry* 48 (1991) 1081–96.

Brown, Brené. *Daring Greatly: How the Courage to Be Vulnerable Transforms the Way We Live, Love, Parent, and Lead*. New York: Gotham, 2012.

Byrd, A. Dean, et al. "Homosexuality: The Innate-Immutability Argument Finds No Basis in Science." *The Salt Lake Tribune* (May 27, 2011) AA6.

Cavinder, Fred D. "Desiderata." *TWA Ambassador* (August 1973) 14–15.

Charlton, T.F. "Fred Phelps and Conservative Christians: Not So Different," *Are Women Human?* (blog), December 24, 2010, http://arewomenhuman.me/2010/12/24/fred-phelps-and-conservative-christians-not-so-different/.

Crabb, Larry. *Fully Alive: A Biblical Vision of Gender That Frees Men and Women to Live Beyond Stereotypes*. Grand Rapids, MI: Baker, 2013.

Crewdson, John. "Study on 'Gay Gene' Challenged." *Chicago Tribune* (June 25, 1995) http://articles.chicagotribune.com/1995-06-25/news/9506250134_1_gay-gene-geneticists-behaviors.

Curtis, Brent, and John Eldredge. *The Sacred Romance: Drawing Closer to the Heart of God*. Nashville: Thomas Nelson, 1997.

Desert Stream/Living Waters Ministries. "History." http://desertstream.org/history/.

———. *Living Waters Support Group Manual*. Grandview, MO: Desert Stream, 2000.

Fagot, B. I. "Beyond the Reinforcement Principle: Another Step Toward Understanding Sex Role Development." *Developmental Psychology* 21 (1985) 1097–104.

Friedman, R. C. *Male Homosexuality: A Contemporary Psychoanalytic Perspective*. New Haven, CT: Yale University Press, 1988.

Friesen, James G., et al. *Living from the Heart Jesus Gave You: The Essentials of Christian Living*. Pasadena, CA: Shepherd's House, 2004.

Hallman, Janelle M. *The Heart of Female Same-Sex Attraction: A Comprehensive Counseling Resource*. Downers Grove, IL: InterVarsity, 2008.

Bibliography

Hamer, Dean, et al. "A Linkage Between DNA Markers on the X Chromosome and Male Sexual Orientation." *Science* 261 (July 1993) 321.

Hu, S., et al. "Linkage Between Sexual Orientation and Chromosome Xq28 in Males But Not in Females." *Nature Genetics* 11 (November 1995) 248–56.

King, Martin Luther, Jr. *Strength to Love.* New York: Harper & Row, 1963.

Kinnaman, David, and Gabe Lyons. *unChristian: What a New Generation Really Thinks about Christianity . . . and Why It Matters.* Grand Rapids, MI: Baker, 2007.

Laaser, Mark R., and Debra Laaser. *The Seven Desires of Every Heart.* Grand Rapids, MI: Zondervan, 2008.

Lee, Justin. *Torn: Rescuing the Gospel from the Gays-vs.-Christians Debate.* New York: Jericho, 2012.

LeVay, Simon. "A Difference in the Hypothalamic Structure Between Heterosexual and Homosexual Men." *Science* 253 (1991) 141–48.

Manning, Brennan. *The Ragamuffin Gospel: Good News for the Bedraggled, Beat-Up, and Burnt Out.* Sisters, OR: Multnomah, 2000.

May, Gerald G. *Addiction and Grace: Love and Spirituality in the Healing of Addictions.* San Francisco: HarperOne, 2007.

Miller, Donald. *Blue like Jazz: Nonreligious Thoughts on Christian Spirituality.* Nashville: Thomas Nelson, 2003.

Nicolosi, Joseph, and Linda Ames Nicolosi. *A Parent's Guide to Preventing Homosexuality.* Downers Grove, IL: InterVarsity, 2002.

Olds, Jacqueline, and Richard Schwartz. *The Lonely American: Drifting Apart in the Twenty-first Century.* Boston: Beacon, 2009.

Paris, Jenell Williams. *The End of Sexual Identity: Why Sex Is Too Important to Define Who We Are.* Downers Grove, IL: InterVarsity, 2011.

Payne, Leanne. *The Broken Image: Restoring Personal Wholeness through Healing Prayer.* Westchester, IL: Cornerstone, 1981.

Platt, Suzy, ed. Respectfully Quoted: A Dictionary of Quotations. Barnes and Noble, 1993.

Scheer, Roddy, and Doug Moss. "Use It and Lose It: The Outsize Effects of U.S. Consumption on the Environment," *EarthTalk* (blog), *Scientific American,* September 14, 2012, http://www.scientificamerican.com/article/american-consumption-habits/.

Schmidt, Thomas E. *Straight & Narrow?: Compassion & Clarity in the Homosexuality Debate.* Downers Grove, IL: IVP Academic, 1995.

Stanford School of Medicine. "Stanford Research into the Impact of Tobacco Advertising." http://tobacco.stanford.edu/tobacco_main/images.php?token2=fm_st298.php&token1=fm_img12128.php&theme_file=fm_mto21.php&theme_name=Targeting%20Doctors&subtheme_name=Icons%20of%20Medicine.

Sweeney, Thomas J. *Adlerian Counseling and Psychotherapy: A Practical Approach for a New Decade,* 3rd ed. Muncie, IN: Accelerated Development, 1989.

Thompson, Curt. *Anatomy of the Soul: Surprising Connections between Neuroscience and Spiritual Practices That Can Transform Your Life and Relationships.* Carol Stream, IL: SaltRiver, 2010.

Timmerman, Tim. *A Bigger World Yet: Faith, Brotherhood, & Same-Sex Needs.* Huron, OH: Bird Dog, 2010.

Vanier, Jean. *From Brokenness to Community.* New York: Paulist, 1992.